Jules Romains's great masterpiece

MEN OF GOOD WILL

"The boldest attempt to describe completely his own time that any French novelist has made since Balzac. Such undertakings are sometimes dangerous, but in the case of Jules Romains, I am convinced that he will succeed, because he has the qualities indispensable for such a task: a perfect technical skill, a deep knowledge of numerous milieus, and (an essential point) an astonishing capacity for work."
—ANDRÉ MAUROIS

THESE ARE BORZOI BOOKS, PUBLISHED BY ALFRED A. KNOPF

SEVEN MYSTERIES
OF EUROPE

SEVEN

MYSTERIES

OF EUROPE

BY

JULES ROMAINS

*Translated from the French
by Germaine Brée*

NEW YORK · ALFRED · A · KNOPF · 1940

CONTENTS

SEVEN MYSTERIES
OF EUROPE

INTRODUCTION

As YOU read my name on the title-page of this book, this is probably what you will say: "Here is a writer straight from Europe, bent on telling us all his pet theories as to the whys and wherefores of what has just happened over there. He may even want to explain with great eloquence how the men in power should have used that power, how the nations should have chosen their leaders, and other splendid tales not entirely unfamiliar to us. Perhaps he wants to give us an account of the events which he, like thousands of others, has witnessed (yes, we have heard about them too!) and which he experienced in his own personal way; or he may have collected exciting anecdotes about the leading characters in the show, and is repeating them for our benefit. Anyway, we can take it or leave it, as we see fit. We are used to that kind of thing by now."

Well, that's just what this book is *not* going to be. It will be something much more specific and occasionally more dramatic. You will soon see why.

The spectacle of the last World War filled me
with horror. I came out of it with one conviction:
We must at all costs avoid any renewal of such atroci-
ties. Many people thought as I thought; thinking,
however, carries no obligation. But this is the vow I
made, a solemn vow, though there were no witnesses
but myself: "I swear I shall always do everything in
my power to prevent the outbreak of another war."

And, you wonder, who was I to make such a vow?
Let me give you some idea. I was still fairly young—
not much more than thirty—I had published a few
books and had already begun to make quite a name
for myself in small literary circles in France and elsewhere. What I said and did seemed of very little
interest to the general public and gave the government little concern.

Try to visualize it in a film: A young, more or less
unknown French writer, walking by himself along
the street, swears he will prevent the next world war.
Touching, yes, but rather ridiculous. But the young
man was not crazy. All that happens in the world
incessantly proves that nothing important is ever
done unless far-reaching plans are made long in advance, at a time when people would laugh if they
heard of them. It all goes to prove, and more and
more clearly, that, in the long run, the most improb-

able and ridiculous plans triumph over the reasonable and moderate ones. The trouble is that we almost always find audacity in conception among gangsters and the enemies of mankind.

I had also given much thought to the way the war had broken loose and to the part played in it by chance. I refused to believe that fatality can determine events. I was convinced that there is always room for an act of will and even of good will; and that the problem lies in the use of the will at the time and in the spot when it can be effective, even if it has very limited means at its disposal.

I could remember, for example, what an enormous effect Zola's *J'accuse* had had in 1897; and I thought of the considerable influence this great writer would have exercised on European opinion, in the cause of peace, if he had been alive in the period between 1905 and 1914.

But as I had a very practical imagination, I considered other forms of action, more personal and direct. I knew that public opinion is one of the great forces in modern society but one which can be misled by men with power and authority, who can distort its reactions and put obstacles in the way of those who wish to reach it. That is why I came to think that to affect events in any way, if you are not in a position of authority, it is not enough to have access to public opinion; you must also have access to those with power and authority and be ready at a decisive moment personally to influence their decisions. I called that: *action on vital points.*

I liked to imagine what a man with the fame of Anatole France might have accomplished during those same years, but an Anatole France on friendly terms with the ministers of foreign affairs and other ministers of state, and who, not limiting himself to exchanging academic opinions with them, would try, with no thought of personal profit, to exercise an influence over them, to share in the problems of state, and to be their adviser, in critical moments. In short, I would try to have some control over actions which usually remain secret and are known to the people only by their results, when it is too late to do anything about them.

Where did I stand fifteen years later? As a writer, I had gained enough authority to make, if need be, a direct appeal to public opinion. But even if such an appeal could still be made in France, a great change had taken place in many other European countries, and there any attempt to reach public opinion was by now a precarious undertaking, and rather ineffective. So my "action on vital points" had become more indispensable than ever before. Since the masses were more and more difficult to reach, it was more and more essential to establish contacts with their masters.

I had been fairly successful in that direction. I was now the friend of a certain number of ranking statesmen both in France and abroad. I tried hard to waste no time; I was not interested in social relations merely for their glamour. I tried to know the people who were really influential or whose importance I could foresee was about to grow. I made it a rule to speak to them freely and on absolutely equal terms. And so it happened that they sometimes told me what was in the back of their minds or, when faced by some great decision, asked for my opinion, and even sent me on missions of extreme consequence which they would not entrust to the usual channels, embassies or legations.

Five years later I had gone still further. One day a man whom in a later chapter I shall call the King's Man (*l'homme du roi*), sent to me by his sovereign, was discussing a vast plan, the existence of which only the three of us knew at the time. He stopped short, glanced around my study, looked me over from head to foot, and exclaimed with a strange laugh: "You know, your position is absolutely unique, in Europe . . . and even in the world. I can't think of any other like it."

And how was that? Just keep this in mind: Men who wield power are used to people seeking their friendship for selfish reasons only. When they meet someone who never has anything to ask for himself, and when they realize that all his efforts are aimed towards a cause of a very high order—national or international—they are surprised and filled with respect. Besides, they are grateful to him for restoring their faith in ideals they once believed in when they were young.

Also, they mistrust people who talk too much. If they tell you a secret, naturally they hate to see it next morning in the papers or to find that everyone is talking about it. They won't make such a mistake again. They knew by experience that they could tell me anything and that nothing would ever leak out.

Yet they would not have taken me into their confidence if they had considered me as nothing more than a dreamer who could not understand the compromises and subtleties involved in political actions. I proved that I could understand, providing the cause was good; and when I had to undertake negotiations myself, that I could take into account every situation and every person.

And then there was another factor in my favour. I was the author of *Men of Good Will*, and almost all the statesmen in Europe had read *Men of Good Will*. Even those who disagreed with the general trend of thought in the book liked the way I spoke of political figures and of their world. The author of such a book was a trusted friend from the start.

And now let me say a word as to how I reconciled

the part I played in my "political" role with the part
I played in the P.E.N. clubs. In the light of conscience
it was not difficult. The P.E.N. clubs, though they
always deny that they are a political association, have
always proclaimed their attachment to such causes as
mutual understanding between nations, peace, and
liberty. I was sure that to use in the service of peace
(therefore of liberty) more effective means than
those at the disposal of literature was to remain faithful in spirit to the P.E.N. clubs. But I kept those two
activities strictly separate and, more specifically, I
never used the authority attached to my title of international president unless I was absolutely sure that I
was working for a universal cause and not only in the
interest of my own country.

I had not planned to say all this until much later, in
my memoirs; and it would have been a tragic story:
"The man who swore he would save peace"—and who
did save it. But a catastrophe has taken place. Europe
lies in ruins, and there is no point in being discreet.
On the contrary, I think it may be helpful to give the
people of the largest democracy still intact a chance
to see clearly through what ineffectual efforts and
weaknesses peace and liberty were lost in Europe.

I must leave many things unsaid, because I have too
much to say, and I shall not tell the tale of my own
experiences in chronological order. They are not

interesting enough just now to deserve public attention. What does deserve it is the mystery of the destiny of Europe, to which my experiences gave me some access, and occasionally allowed me to penetrate, or about which I can at least form acceptable hypotheses.

These revelations and explanations may, for obvious reasons, bring denials. I ask my readers not to be disturbed by them; I have added nothing to the truth.

I

THE MYSTERY OF DALADIER

I saw him coming towards me, his hand outstretched; a man of my own age, shorter than I, stockily built, bull-necked; a typical Gallo-Roman face; a dull brown complexion, sharp eyes, a southern voice, distinct and energetic.

"I've read your play," he said. "Come and sit down. I don't usually like political plays—Romain Rolland's, for example. I'd been told they were remarkably good; they seem to me empty and declamatory. You give your politicians the right mentality and put them face to face with real situations and problems. A fine play! The ladies and gentlemen of the Comédie-Française assure me they like it very much but don't dare take the responsibility of producing it, because of the politics in it—and add that I alone can do it. All right, I will. If the performance causes any trouble and I am asked why I gave the Comédie-Française permission to put on your *Dictator,* I'll mount the tribune and tell them why."

I had been summoned by Daladier. It was in the spring of 1926. The committee of the Comédie-Française (composed of actors, with the administrator as chairman), to which I had submitted my play *The Dictator,* had accepted it "unanimously and with congratulations," only to declare almost immediately that it was impossible to act the play, because of the political demonstrations it might stir up in the audience. Now, the Comédie-Française, the leading state-subsidized theatre, feared censorship as little as any other theatre, but it felt obliged to protect its magnificence by all sorts of precautions. Besides, it was bound to the political world by ties which had to be dealt with tactfully. Many of the young actresses were on the most intimate terms with ministers of state or members of Parliament.

We spoke of the administrator of the Comédie-Française, a man notorious for his lack of backbone and famous for his mixture of weakness and cunning. "When he comes to see me," Daladier said with a laugh, "he never takes his eyes off the door, as if he were making ready to run." Then: "I've been bored stiff lately by his tale of three young actresses, all without talent, whom he took against his better judgment, merely because they happened to be the mistresses of some minister or former minister. He came here to weep on my shoulder, but naturally he never would have had the courage to refuse these ladies when they were forced on him."

And more generally: "It's just as bad everywhere else; the most influential civil servants complain that *Timidity* some minister or politician exercises pressure on them. If any one of them had enough courage to say perfectly calmly: 'You have come to ask me to do something contrary both to my sense of duty and to the interests of the country, and I can show you why,' nine times out of ten the minister would withdraw his request and regard the other man with quite new respect." And he laughed again. "I must say I can speak with complete detachment. I've never had a mistress among the young women of the Comédie, and that, of course, for a Minister of Public Instruction, is most extraordinary." He went on: "I saw exactly the same kind of thing when I was Minister of Colonies. You can't imagine the type of 'feudal lords' the Minister of Colonies has to deal with. If he once fails to look them squarely in the face, he is done for."

As I left him I thought: "Here is a man." And a little later: "Perhaps he is the man we are hoping for, the man we need so badly. I'll try not to lose sight of him."

A few months later he was no longer a minister, but the Radical-Socialist Party had elected him to be its president. The Radical-Socialist Party was still the most powerful governing party in France, and its president a man who could, if he so wished, exercise the strongest influence over French politics both inside and outside France. It was time now that France should set out on the path towards social reform and the creation of a permanent order in Europe. I wrote to Daladier: "A double task lies ahead of us: we must incorporate syndicalism into the state, and we must build the unity of Europe. Our success depends largely on you." Daladier answered that he was greatly honoured by the faith I put in him and hoped he would prove worthy of it.

You have all seen the Place de la Concorde, if only in the movies. And now picture it on a February evening, a very soft, dry evening. Thousands of people have gathered in the square—waiting for fireworks perhaps, or some great procession? No, for they are all much too tense. As they talk, watch their gestures. Many of the men are wearing the *béret basque* and they carry walking-sticks. Now and then the crowd in the square begins to swirl and a few score people surge forward, shouting. There are occasional revolver shots, but in so large a space they sound thin and ludicrous, like children's firecrackers. Against the distant Pont de la Concorde I can distinguish clearly a line of cavalry. They advance towards the

14

centre of the square and try to sweep the crowd in front of them as they come. But there are only sixteen of them, or twenty at most; in fan formation they advance very slowly, with difficulty, and that, too, seems ludicrous. I hear a tense voice close to me: "We don't know what to do, we have no orders." Later that evening there were more violent movements in the crowd; revolvers were fired more often. Then, somewhere over in the direction of the bridge, we heard something that sounded like a salvo—the Garde Républicaine, or the Garde Mobile perhaps, had fired.

That was the famous riot of February 6, 1934.

At midnight I was still in the Place de la Concorde. What I saw was still as incomprehensible and absurd. It was said that some people had been killed, but no one seemed able to figure out who the leaders of the mob might be, what their aim was, or exactly what they hoped to gain by it.

I felt one thing only, very clearly; it was a terrible impression: the authority of the state lay there discarded, torn to bits like an old newspaper. I could not sense anywhere the presence of authority or of any organic force. It seemed as if Paris in its nocturnal vastness were abandoned, left face to face with dire confusion and dismay.

Now, that evening Daladier, the Daladier I had spoken to eight years before, was the man in power.

15

Over and over again, desperately, I repeated to myself that I could not understand. He had come into power once again a fortnight before, called back and acclaimed by public opinion, heralded by a legend, the legend which had slowly taken shape during those eight years: a strong man, silent, stubborn, with an energetic thrust to his chin, bull-necked—the "Vaucluse bull"—a man who had never been in a hurry, who had not tried to exhaust in one venture all the hopes placed upon him, a man whose career lay ahead of him, and who therefore could afford to wait for great events. And now surely, within a few weeks, he would punish sedition, reduce to silence factious organizations, bring order back into the streets. Yet at midnight on that 6th of February I could hear the men around me in the Place de la Concorde say: "In any case Daladier must go; we've had enough of him." I could not understand.

At one o'clock I walked into a tobacco shop in the avenue Marceau. There I bought a *carte pneumatique*; on one side I wrote: "M. Édouard Daladier, President of the Council," and on the other: "Whatever happens, hold on. This riot is absolutely unimportant. A little energy, and you can save freedom in the Republic."

Next day there was a rumour that Daladier's Cabinet had resigned, "because it would not spill French blood." On the night of February 7, buses were

16

burned in the streets, and organized groups went around in trucks, looting the shops. Policemen stood by quietly watching them. And everywhere scowling men repeated: "Death to Daladier, the Executioner!"

What a blow for me! The man in whom I had placed so much confidence and seen such inexhaustible reserves of cool-headedness and energy had capitulated before an insignificant riot, which could not even have got under way if only he had taken the most simple precautionary police measures. He could abandon Paris to the scum of the population and leave France at the mercy of civil war; because of a few miserable shots fired, without orders, by the Garde Mobile the evening before, in the general tension, he was now condemned to carry for years the name "Daladier the Executioner."

It was long before I regained the confidence so brutally destroyed. I could see that, put to the test in great circumstances, Daladier's personality—his political personality, I mean—had suddenly revealed a deep flaw. It took too large a dose of optimism to hope that the flaw might disappear and, what was more important still, not reappear under a similar blow.

Two years later the elections in May 1936 resulted in a large majority for the Popular Front. It was clear that the Popular Front (with Daladier as one of its leaders, though a somewhat timorous leader, of secondary importance) was coming into power. And what is more, a government formed by the Popular Front had such an overwhelming majority in Parliament that it might quite conceivably stay in power for the whole duration of the new legislature—till 1940.

The European situation was becoming steadily worse. Nazi Germany was growing day by day in strength and insolence. Fascist Italy, offended by the Ethiopian question, was moving towards Germany. (I will tell you later how the democracies, at that moment, let slip a unique occasion to save peace and freedom in the world.)

In foreign affairs the Popular Front lacked both preparation and ideas, though in this field Léon Blum was both well informed and intelligent; but he would always be checked and handicapped by the Communists, taking their orders from Moscow. He needed, to support him, a non-Marxist as Minister of Foreign Affairs, a man independent, with sound common sense, absolutely honest, profoundly attached to the cause of peace, and determined not to be drawn into all kinds of adventures just to please the Communists. There were not many to choose from.

And I now admit quite openly that I used political intrigue to place in the position of Minister of Foreign Affairs a man who, in my opinion, was well fitted for the job; but no one at the time had thought of him for

18

the post: Yvon Delbos. Léon Jouhaux, who was all-powerful then in his position as general secretary of the International Confederation of Labour, and who had just refused a portfolio in the new Cabinet, helped me with my plan. I only mentioned it to Delbos when things were well under way. He seemed a little taken aback, but he finally admitted: "Well, after all, I think I'd like it." A few days later, when I was in New York (I was to spend the summer in the States), I learned with pleasure that my little plan had worked, and that Delbos was at the Quai d'Orsay.

Meanwhile Daladier had accepted the Ministry of War. "So," I thought, "they are giving him another chance. After all, he must have some of the qualities we attributed to him. He will be able to work in peace, surrounded by technicians. Our soldiers must be kept in good condition, out of the reach of demagogues. He may succeed. He must have had plenty of time to meditate the lesson he learned on February 6."

At the beginning of 1938 Daladier became president of the council and kept the Ministry of War. Georges Bonnet took the place of Delbos at the Quai d'Orsay (after a short passage of Paul-Boncour, during the precarious second Blum Cabinet).

I kept as closely in touch with Georges Bonnet as previously with Delbos, and for the same reasons: to fend off most carefully any occasion for war, while grouping and consolidating every chance of peace. It was then that I undertook a vast journey through fourteen European countries, a journey in which I was to investigate, through confidential and detailed discussions with the masters of Europe (rulers, ministers, leaders of public opinion), what chances still remained to preserve peace in Europe by forming a union of the free nations—or those that were still partly free.

Quite naturally, in my talks with Georges Bonnet, I had always inquired: "You are keeping Daladier informed, of course? What is his opinion?" But with Georges Bonnet (most unfairly criticized, I believe, in France and elsewhere, and on whom, pending further information,[1] I can bestow nothing but praise) my conversations were so substantial and so rich in concrete results that on the whole I had no urge to go and tell Daladier what I felt sure Georges Bonnet was telling him all along.

Again, when in June 1938 I was asked to tell certain things to President Beneš, in Prague, Georges Bonnet said to me before I took my leave: "Why, certainly, Monsieur Daladier is in complete agreement with us. You can speak plainly."

I would sometimes ask Georges Bonnet: "How is he right now?"

"Well. . . ."

---

[1] Cf. Chapter VII.

"Full of courage? Cheerful?"

"Yes. My impression is that he sees things exactly as we do."

One day, at the very beginning of November, a very worried Georges Bonnet said to me:

"The Premier is in a rather dangerous mood."

It was exactly one month after Munich. Daladier came back from Munich sure that he had done his best, but terribly anxious. He thought that Parisians would greet him with jeers, and instead, from the time he stepped out of the plane on to the rue Saint-Dominique, he was greeted by the most enthusiastic ovations; and for Daladier the next few days were days of perfect bliss. Then came a very sudden change of opinion. People began to wonder whether Munich had not been a complete sell-out. A speech Hitler made at Saarbrücken further cooled all enthusiasm. In the lobbies of Parliament, intrigues flourished anew. The Communists, who had orders from Moscow to spike the Daladier-Bonnet Cabinet as a punishment for Munich, started, in the cleverest and most treacherous manner, to stir up trouble in the working classes (and even the war, a year later, put no end to their activities).

"Yes," said Bonnet to me, "and there are more serious things even than that. One is that Daladier takes it so to heart. He feels he is threatened on all sides.

21

He does not realize his enormous popularity with those who are the backbone of the country. With a little energy, he could sweep away all intriguers and force the Communist agitators to run to cover. But he is capable of weakness, and if he weakens, all is lost."

I agreed absolutely. We spoke, more fully than ever before, about the case of Daladier. We both thought that he very probably might not be one of those great statesmen who can save a country by the force of their own genius. But everything at the time tended to give the impression that he was a great statesman. Once again people had placed immense hopes in him (no one remembered now his collapse of February 7, 1934), and that made him almost as useful to France in danger as one of the real heroes of our political history—or at least it made him almost as necessary. He was literally irreplaceable. If he went, it would mean the worst muddle in Parliament, unrest in factories and streets, the beginning of anarchy, and within a few weeks foreign invasion.

"Now listen," Bonnet told me, "you should go and have a long talk with him. What we try to say to him to bolster him up has little effect now. You alone can speak to him in a certain way and give him the moral jolt he needs to pull himself together. But act quickly."

I thought hard. I remembered the card I had sent

22

the night of February 6. It made me smile, but still I answered Bonnet:

"All right, I can always try; but don't forget that, in a conversation, you may or may not be inspired; and if you don't strike quickly and hard, you fail. I should like to write him, after weighing my words carefully, as moving a letter as I know how, and put off seeing him until later. I hope by then the letter will have had its effect. A conversation will do the rest."

"A good idea. Write that letter as soon as you can. I'll take it to him myself, and make sure that nobody but him opens it."

We were both thinking of his entourage—not bad people, but inclined already to cut him off rather jealously from the rest of the world.

On November 4 I handed Georges Bonnet a letter, which he took immediately to Daladier. Here is a faithful copy of the text:

Paris, Nov. 4, 1938.
134 Fbg. St. Honoré

Monsieur le Président:

I wish to put into this letter all the gravity and all the force of persuasion of which I am capable.

I beseech you to consider at this hour the whole extent of your duty and of your power.

You can still, in the next few days, save France and her present form of government from the fate which otherwise awaits her and which I need not point out to you, for you see it quite clearly.

Your credit with the nation is immense. You have had countless evidences of it, but you still are likely to under-estimate it. Whereas others get excited so easily and fool themselves, you have always had within yourself to con-tend with the relentless questionings of a scrupulous mind; that morally is all to your credit—that is why you are liked. But it is also what now you must overcome.

But such enormous credit will not be invested in your name much longer. You can now ask of France almost everything within reason that can be asked of her. But if you don't obtain it immediately and completely, France will slide right back into political infirmity and catas-trophe. And worst of all for men like ourselves, it will mean that no one, either in the élite of the nation or among the masses, will have enough courage left to defend the republican régime (and this for the first time since it was established).

You are the only man who can pull us out of this, for reasons unequal in value, some of them purely acciden-tal. But the fact remains, and we yield before it; and you also must yield. The man you are and the man fashioned by circumstances are now one—indissoluble and at pres-ent irreplaceable. But it would be tragic if the man you are did not realize all this with the full consciousness and inner tension that are necessary for the part you must play.

If you are thorough in your actions and push on *to the end,* you are almost sure of success; and even failure would make you appear greater before your own conscience and before history.

If you take half-measures, if you try to spare this man or that, if you are too slow and cautious, you are sure to fail; you will leave behind you an impossible situation in which everything will be left to despair and chance.

In short, this is the decisive hour in your destiny. It is not possible to speak of all this without using solemn words. This is no longer the time to be merely a statesman and do your job as a statesman honourably. You are compelled to greatness and heroism.

You need no one to tell you what you must do. Advisers can be of no use to you, even the most venerable old pontiffs. They are too old and too slow to cope with events; and when their false wisdom will have caused the ruin of our country and the fall of the regime, they will go groaning into exile and fill American magazines with retrospective *"mea culpas"*.

I beseech you to listen to your own self—yes, listen to your "voices". At the bottom of your heart, you will always be a republican, a democrat, a son of the people, not content to give mere lip service to the French Republic, but determined from the bottom of your heart to save it. And so doing, you will further immeasurably the great cause of democracy throughout the world. You will give it a new value.

> Faithfully yours,
> *Jules Romains*

In a postscript I added that I was leaving that night

for England and would be back on the 11th. As soon as I got back, he sent for me.

I walked into his office, in the rue Saint-Dominique, and saw before me the same man as in the spring of 1926—a little fatter, his face redder and slightly heavier, with kind, rather tired-looking eyes, but still very keen, and the same voice as before. He held out both hands.

"Your letter did me good, Jules Romains."

We spoke freely, in complete understanding. We went over all the dangers in the situation, at home and abroad. I gave him some impressions and news from England which agreed with the trend of my letter:

"You can count on me," he said. "I swear that I know the full extent of my responsibility before history. I shall try to prove equal to my task. I shall not betray your faith in me, nor lose the faith and confidence placed in me by men like you."

As for myself, I felt full of affection and almost tenderness for the man who had to bear the weight of such a destiny. I said:

"There will probably be difficult moments ahead, and if you ever need me . . ."

He pondered awhile. I liked the grave expression on his face as he thought—standing there, staring at the floor, his head slightly sunk in his shoulders.

"Listen," he said, "in a few days—not now, but I will let you know, when the things I fear are more threatening—you might make an Appeal to the Nation. I'll have it broadcast by all the radio stations, and I'll keep my eyes open on account of a certain number of petty botchers who sabotage all they can."

"All right."

A week later he called me in. The danger had increased. Parliamentary trouble-makers were preparing the decisive onslaught to overthrow the Cabinet, while the Communists were plotting a general strike for the end of the month. In Italy demonstrations against France were being organized, as a prelude to more serious manœuvres. Germany seemed little anxious to push a plan for "a joint Franco-German declaration" which was to be the logical sequel to Munich on the way to appeasement, and no one knew to what extent she secretly encouraged Italy's game.

I wrote that "Appeal to the Nation" and put my whole heart into it. On the 23rd, without showing it to Daladier, I informed him that I would deliver it on the 24th at half past eight in the evening. He said:

"I am having dinner at the British Embassy with Mr. Neville Chamberlain. But don't worry, we shall all be listening to you."

My Appeal was received with immense enthusiasm throughout the nation. There were a few insults from the Communists, but I got innumerable letters, all ardently friendly, from the very heart of the nation:

humble employees, school-teachers, workers, peasants. It was made into a pamphlet and hundreds of
thousands of copies were distributed. In all sincerity
I believe that it helped Daladier's position in the
country and had a good deal to do with the failure
of the general strike on the 30th of November. But
on the 24th the instigators of the strike had gone too
far to give it up.

The order to strike was given to all the workers in
the country, including all civil servants and railroad
employees. Germany, shrouded in enigmatic silence,
was waiting to see what would happen. The Fascist
extremists—forcing Mussolini's hand more perhaps
than he wanted—were already organizing their famous
demonstration for the evening just before the strike:
"Tunisia! Corsica! Savoia! Nizza!"

I thought with anxiety: "Let us hope that this time
Daladier won't weaken as on February 7!"

Two days before the date for which the strike was
called, Daladier took measures which were a tribute
to his great energy and determination: all railroad
employees were mobilized, and therefore liable to be
court-martialled if they deserted. Any civil servant,
from the highest to the lowest, who did not turn up
at his job on the morning of November 30 would be
dismissed. There would be large concentrations of
police and Gardes Mobiles.

But I was still afraid of one thing. I was aware that *Regards strike of Nov 30 1938* in Parliament there were plenty of weak-kneed politicians who were urging Daladier to "talk" with the Communist agitators. I knew that some of the ministers were working along the same line, thus showing *3* once more a most incredible blindness. And I thought: "The same thing must have happened on the 6th and 7th of February 1934. . . . Someone should have been there on the 7th to keep Daladier from weakening and to comfort him with the presence of one who was not panicky."

On the evening of the 29th I sent him the following note:

My dear Premier:

Your energy is admirable. All the measures you have taken are excellent. Now hang on and don't give in on a single point. I think the blackest moment will come at eleven o'clock tomorrow morning. I wish to be with you at that time so that you will feel you are not alone. Don't take the trouble to send an answer. At eleven I shall knock at the door of your office.

Next morning, at eleven o'clock sharp, I walked into Daladier's office. He rose from behind his desk. His face was calm and radiant.

"I did hang on, Jules Romains. It's over and I won." He showed me the papers on his desk. "Here are the first figures. The proportion of strikers is ridiculous. The strike is a fiasco. . . . A minute ago a

29

friend of mine who was near the Ternes telephoned to say everyone was working in the most spectacular way." He laughed gaily at the word "spectacular"; then he went on:

"It is not because I lacked advice from timid souls. Just think, Jules Romains, yesterday afternoon four of my ministers—yes, four—came into this office to beseech me to negotiate with the leaders of the Communist agitation. . . . As you see, I took no one's advice." He continued, emphasizing each word: "Now I can afford to be magnanimous. I shall try to dismiss as few of them as possible. . . . I shall ask the employers, forcefully if need be, not to take advantage of my victory."

I must admit that the thought given to magnanimity at that moment, by a man whose victory might have gone to his head, for a few hours at least, seemed to me to bear the mark of real nobility and to be worthy of admiration.

From that day on, my relations with Daladier were most affectionate and friendly. True to my principle of not disturbing people who are busy working—as I am a hard worker myself—I never saw him except when necessary; but it was always with pleasure, a pleasure shared by him, I feel sure.

For example, on December 12, 1938 he came to my house, in the rue du Faubourg Saint-Honoré, to dinner. We had planned a party, my wife and I, to give him the feeling that the finest elements of the intellectual élite in France were with him, stood behind him, encouraged him. We had invited people like Paul Valéry, Paul Morand, Jacques Copeau, and their wives, Henri Bonnet, head of the Institute for Intellectual Co-operation, and charming Hellé Bonnet, his wife, François Porché and Simone. We had invited the André Maurois, who were sorry they could not be in Paris at that time. The Prefect of Police, Langeron, was with us, and indeed deserved to be there as a most delightful man and as a friend of writers and artists. And we also had Georges Bonnet, the Minister of Foreign Affairs, and his wife.

If I dwell on this dinner party now, it is because I cannot think of it without emotion. First because of the brilliance of the guests and the exciting quality of the remarks Daladier and Bonnet improvised for such an exceptional audience. Then, also, because of two strange incidents. The butler suddenly appeared: *"Monsieur le Préfet de Police* is wanted on the telephone."

Langeron rose and after a minute came back and said in his usual unruffled way, with his imperturbable smile:

"There is a fire at the Invalides. I must go and see what is happening. Will you excuse me?"

Then he added:

"Now Premier Daladier is wanted on the telephone."

Daladier rose in his turn, and a minute later came back to the dining-room to present his excuses to my wife:

"Madame Romains, I am very sorry indeed. Langeron just said there was a fire at the Invalides, but my chief secretary informs me that there is a fire at the Palais-Bourbon—well, hardly a fire, but a very stormy session—they are demanding a vote of confidence. . . . I had a majority of only seven this morning. I run serious risk of being overthrown if I don't rush there right away."

Here is another example: In April 1939 I was about to leave for the United States to attend the World Congress of Writers. I called on Daladier to ask if he had a message he would like me to take to America.

"Tell the Americans we never for one instant wish to drag them with us into a war. . . . All we ask of them is that they help us prevent war. . . . You can tell them that, for it's the plain truth. . . . And tell President Roosevelt too, if you see him. But how well he knows it!"

Then he added, in a more confidential tone:

"President Roosevelt would like to see us get through the next two or three months without any incidents that could give Hitler the slightest pretext for attacking us; he thinks that these months are going

to be the most dangerous for all the European democracies, because of the still considerable lag in armaments which we have to make up."

Daladier wanted then, with all his heart, just what
he had wanted on the eve of Munich: to preserve
peace. I can swear to it. In the chapter devoted to
the mystery of Leopold III I shall bring forward more
proofs attesting the feelings of the French government at that time.

It was Monday, October 16, 1939, and almost
noon. I was in Brussels in the office of the French
Ambassador.

The war was six weeks old. Daladier now practically had full dictatorial powers. He held three port-
folios himself. The other ministers took his orders,
listened when he explained, but were never consulted
on the general policies of the government.

I had come to Brussels to fulfil a mission which
seemed very important to me. Now, as I look back,
it seems more important than ever. I shall say more
about it in the chapter on "The Mystery of Leopold
III." I had not kept the Ambassador completely informed, as Paris had given me full liberty to act as I
saw fit. But he knew that in case of need he must place
himself completely at my disposition.

I said:

"I want Paris immediately on the telephone."

"I'll see you get it myself. And in Paris whom shall we call?"

"Premier Daladier."

The Ambassador jumped.

"You are perfectly sure I can ask for him?"

I saw then that by now the Premier seemed to him an unapproachable divinity.

As we were waiting for the connection, the Ambassador warned me to be cautious:

"Choose your words with care. The line is tapped, and God knows what ears the slightest indiscretion reaches."

The telephone rang. I picked up the receiver.

"Hello, is that you, Jules Romains? From where are you calling?"

"From Brussels, from the Embassy. . . . It is absolutely necessary that I see you tomorrow afternoon and that you give me some time. I have serious things to tell you."

"Would three o'clock be all right?"

"I cannot leave until tomorrow morning on the express. It is very often late."

"One minute. How about five o'clock?"

"Right. But would you be so kind as to see me at five o'clock sharp, because, under the circumstances, I really ought to leave for Brussels the same evening on the night train?"

"All right. I'll manage."

On the train I kept going over in my head the little speech I had prepared for Daladier. I wanted to get a decision out of him within five minutes. I was still carried along by the activity and energy I had shown in my six-day fight with the Belgian government.

All those who were in contact with Daladier—his ministers, for instance—had been saying since the declaration of war: "It is impossible to get any decision from him. He thinks too much." And: "He is more and more inaccessible. . . . You can't ask him for a five-minute interview without lending yourself to all kinds of complications, and he is becoming extremely suspicious."

I was ushered in at a few minutes past five. I hardly took time to inquire how he was or to look at him. I noticed, however, that his face was very red and his eyes dull.

"I have just arrived from Brussels, as you know. After six days of incessant work—hard going most of the time—I want to inform you of the results, which seem to me of great importance and which we hardly dared hope to obtain a week ago."

I enumerated them in a few rapid sentences.

". . . But now we must immediately consolidate them. This is the plan M. Spaak and I agreed on.

You will give me a letter in your own handwriting for the King. . . ."

"For the King?" He looked at me intently, with suspicion.

"Yes. We even agreed, M. Spaak and I, on the wording of the letter. We have the King's approval; the scenario is ready. I shall go back to Brussels to-night. The King will give me an audience tomorrow and I'll deliver the letter. He will give me his answer, which I'll bring back to you. And there we are. From then on, their word is pledged."

Daladier's expression was inscrutable, almost harsh. First he tried to show me, by a few chilling comments, that the aforementioned results were far less important than I seemed to think—that he, Daladier, had always considered them as already established, and obvious.

I was thunderstruck. No one could know better than I did what the situation really was at that time, nor what the general attitude of the Belgian government had been before and after the six days I had just spent there. I knew far too well all the difficulties I had been through, and I could still see all too clearly the almost scared look in M. Spaak's face as I drew from him the last cautious concession.

Was Daladier afraid that I might give too much importance to the part I had played in this affair? Did he wish me to believe that he had foreseen everything and, at such a distance, directed everything? I was struck by another peculiarity. He could no longer listen. He never asked a single question about those six days during which I had gathered such a store of impressions and information; worse still, when I tried to explain some situation or other in the most concise terms, he would interrupt me to give the explanation before I could, as a proof, I suppose, that he knew it all better than I did. (I couldn't help thinking of Maykosen and William II in *Men of Good Will*.)

But I am not a person to be discouraged by such details. I renewed my efforts:

"In any event, I must go back tonight, with the letter."

"Certainly not tonight. I am working with Gamelin till past midnight."

"But, with your permission, I shall go into another room. I'll make a draft of the letter, since we definitely agreed on the terms. It won't take you five minutes to copy it in your own hand and sign it."

He shook his head.

"No. First, because I can't write to the King of the Belgians."

"Why not?"

"Because I am not the head of the state. It's up to President Lebrun to write that letter. . . . And just think of the complications involved."

"But, my dear Premier, I must beseech you! Remember we are at war, that Belgium and Holland may be attacked within the next week! That this matter is urgent and of the most prodigious importance! And if this is not the time to abandon your formalities, can you think of a better? Since the King approves! He is the only one who might be embarrassed."

"I'll think it over, I promise you."

As he accompanied me to the door of his office, slowly, hesitatingly, and obviously with some reluctance, I tried to make an appeal to his pride:

"The King, who is, after all, still a young man, has a deep admiration for you and esteems you highly."

"I know—I know. . . ." (So! He knew even that beforehand.)

". . . A letter, written by you, and by no one else, that is what will flatter him, impress him. A letter I will deliver myself in these unusual circumstances. . . . You remember what he asked me to do for him last year. All these details will fire his imagination. We must keep everything on the same dramatic plane."

We shook hands, and he answered:

"I told you I shall think it over. I'll send Coulondre my decision. Go and see him tomorrow at the Quai d'Orsay."

Next day Coulondre said to me: "The Premier is still undecided. . . . He says we must not be in such a hurry. . . . In his words: 'We'll let them simmer for a while.'"

I could not let it go at that. The stakes were too high. Since I had not managed to gain Daladier's approval by a direct assault, I decided to organize a siege. I called successively on Georges Bonnet, then Minister of Justice, on my old friend Delbos, Minister of National Instruction, on Paul Reynaud, Minister of Finance. They all repeated in almost exactly the same words:

"Evidently it's of great importance and it's absurd to keep the King waiting. . . . We'll see if we can speak to Daladier. . . . But that's very difficult. He doesn't like us to question him on such matters unless he himself has mentioned them first—and, actually, he never mentions them. . . . Why don't you try to see someone of his entourage? Clapier, for example."

I went to see Clapier. He received me cordially, understood what I wanted, and promised to do something about it.

But I did not go back to Brussels until three months later. And the King never got Daladier's letter.

I could describe other aspects of Daladier during the war. They would add nothing essential to the scene I have just depicted.

And now we may ask: What was his basic worth? What kind of man had he become?

ing was in
1939

He had become, in fact, a dictator. He had all the power of dictatorship, but none of its efficiency. Yet, in his soul, he was still a democrat. I am convinced that he regarded his dictatorship as a temporary obligation forced on him by circumstances. He longed for the day when he could declare to the Parliament of a victorious France: "There! We have once again assured the triumph of the ideal of republican France and of human liberty. I feel proud that you should be satisfied with what I did. Let me go and rest."

Yes, he was a dictator, but his effectiveness was handicapped first of all by certain deficiencies of character. The Daladier of February 6 had not quite disappeared, though he had learned how to stiffen his words against sudden collapse; he had given way to certain paralysing inclinations, a tendency to sink into interminable meditation, procrastination, and endless indecision. But he had a worse handicap: he was a dictator hampered by a democratic conscience. That must be said, for it is all to his honour. He could not find sufficient strength to shatter the resistance that surrounded him arising from the red tape and routine of the democratic machine, nor to give the necessary jolt to indolence, inertia, and criminal compromise. He could not find that strength because he was always stopped by the scruples of a free man, afraid to use free men as mere tools. He could respect even the ceremonial formalities.

40

Unfortunately this had not prevented him from contracting almost unconsciously many of the vices of dictators: suspicion of others, a taste for solitude, the fixed notion that he was always right and knew everything, a rising aversion for strong and independent characters who might speak to him as equals and say: "You are wrong."

A very grave and very disconcerting question is the following: How did he see this war? Did he wage it so badly because he was unable to see it clearly?

It remains mysterious in part. But I think there is an answer that towers above the mystery and throws light on it from above.

Daladier always hated war from the bottom of his heart. He had fought in the last war as a simple soldier. One of the fixed ideas of his political career had certainly been: "We shall never again throw our country into a war like that one. We'll know how to manage better than our predecessors. If, in the end, they let themselves be drawn into war, it was because they did not hate war with our sincerity."

Right up to March 15, 1939 he believed that he could manage it. That's why he agreed to Munich. I saw him when he began to realize that it might conceivably no longer be possible to manage, because our enemies wanted war at all costs. And even then he still clung to some hope; he expected a last-minute miracle.

When the war broke out, I am sure he thought: "How absurd!" but millions of us could not get rid of that same absurd, confused idea: "Who knows? Perhaps it will drag on and on and fail. We may beat Germany either by internal revolution or through her weariness or a psychological and economic collapse. No blood will be spilled, or hardly any. And the world will start to breathe freely again."

That is probably not a very good state of mind in which to carry on war; and it is with sadness and regret that I point it out to democrats in every land, and to all the friends of peace and liberty.

You may say: "But that does not explain why during the many years when he was Minister of National Defence he did not build planes and tanks. It is no excuse for his lack of vigilance during the first six months of the war about such matters as training the army, the intensive production of equipment, the setting up of a completely modern system of defence, taking into account the methods applied first in Poland, then in Finland."

No, certainly not.

Allusions, more or less veiled, have been made to his intemperate habits. People said that to pep himself up he kept drinking more and more apéritifs, making them stiffer and stiffer. That may be true; but I don't think it was ever a decisive factor.

Others mention women—one especially: the Mar-

42

quise de Crussol. I am afraid it is a fact that Daladier wasted too much time and energy in that direction. I am also sorry that the son of the Carpentras baker fell such an easy prey to snobbism in his liaison with a marquise. But what was worse, he exposed himself thus to influences at best questionable and more often definitely pernicious. I consider that factor, however, as also of secondary importance.

Women, I think, had much less influence in all this than the generals. Daladier, the democrat, former president of the Radical-Socialist Party, once leader of the Popular Front, the sworn enemy of war and militarism, had slowly turned into the faithful servant of the generals. His failures and resentments had led him to shut himself up in the Ministry of War as in a monastery; and there the men with whom he was in daily contact were almost all generals, the advice he heard was almost always voiced by army men. And he found them charming, for, contrary to the current opinion, their voices are measured, cautious, even insinuating, and convey respect, devotion, and sometimes affection.

This brings us to the mystery of Gamelin.

II

THE MYSTERY OF GAMELIN

IF, as some people claim, an experience is of no value unless it is progressive, then my experience with generals is not worth much, for what it lacked most was a gradual development.

For many years I added nothing to what I had learned formerly as a private, for whom an infantry sergeant represented the familiar horizon which he dared look at without too much uneasiness but not without fear. The captain was a far-distant peak. As for the general, he was a kind of Gaurisankar, hidden behind clouds and quite fantastic.

Now, it so happened that since the days of my infantry sergeants the first officer with whom I came in contact was Weygand, then general inspector of army, and generalissimo designate in time of war. (That was less than seven years ago.)

As I come to think of it, that sounds a little too sim-
plified. Surely, in embassies, in the course of my
travels through Europe, I must have come across some
generals. But in embassies the species is unusually
well tamed and inoffensive. I had never thought of
drawing any conclusions on the subject, any more
than I would flatter myself that I knew all about the
primitive life of Indian tribes just because at the
Grand Canyon I had watched the Indian war dance
on the terrace in front of the hotel.

So I met Weygand, at a lunch given by friends of
mine. Our host had been careful to warn us. General
Weygand had expressed some apprehensions. "I
hear," he said, "that your Romains is such a Leftist!"
"No, no! Wait and see—he is broad-minded, and takes
an interest in everything. . . ."
After lunch, while coffee was being served, we were
left alone in the garden so that we could talk privately.
Unaccustomed to such privileges, I should have felt
dizzy. Luckily I discovered immediately several of
the traits peculiar to generals, which become more
and more accentuated the higher you go in the
hierarchy: exquisite courtesy, affability, deference
towards their interlocutor—the total impression given
being one of unassuming modesty, almost like a young
girl's (and I must say I know few girls nowadays who
aren't bolder and capable of interrupting and con-

tradicting in more peremptory tones). As Weygand and I exchanged the first few remarks, I recalled out of the past the figure of a certain sergeant with whom I had found it much less easy to get on, and thought: "If Sergeant Gamonet were here, I guess we'd be in for quite a bad time of it, Weygand and I."

I gave him no time to start talking about literature. I spoke to him about what he was doing, which just then seemed more interesting to me. I remember asking him almost immediately what part he thought aviation would play in the next war. Don't think that was a proof of exceptional foresight; all I had done was to read magazine articles written by specialists. Their authors claimed that the progress made in aviation would alter existing conditions of warfare to such a degree that it would be folly to rely on large numbers of troops. In particular there was a great deal of talk about the theories of an Italian general named Douhet. In France some politicians—Leftists and even extreme Leftists, which is worth mentioning—contended that the money necessary to lengthen the term of compulsory service could be put to much better use in the creation of a formidable air force. Others warned us that Germany, though she had not the right to build warplanes, was turning out large commercial ships which could very easily be transformed into bombers. So it was quite natural that since I had the Supreme Commander of the French Army right there, I should seize the opportunity to get his opinion. He answered in carefully measured tones:

"Such ideas are certainly not negligible. But aviation cannot carry the decision; to carry the decision you must take possession of the field, and the air force can never take possession of the field."

He said other plausible things about how essential it was for the air force to have bases at a suitable distance from the firing line, and about the limitations arising from this. He did not say that the infantry would always "reign supreme in battle." He did not repeat old-fashioned clichés of that type. But he left me with the impression that he did not believe that modern mechanized equipment was going to revolutionize both tactics and strategy.

I also found out the same day—though he spoke of it not to me, but to someone else—that he would soon reach the age limit, but would do absolutely nothing to cling to his position, convinced that the regulation which provided for the advancement of young officers was basically sound. There was merit in his acceptance of the regulation, for he had preserved his trim figure and an unmistakable vigour and elasticity of muscle such as most men manage to lose by the time they are thirty. You could easily picture him riding his thirty miles on horseback. And that's exactly why, when we separated, I said: "How fascinating the man is—quite perfect! I can detect nothing of the 'Colonel

Blimp' about him—" and yet I added under my breath: "Let's hope he hasn't the slightest tinge of 'cavalier' mentality!" This, in my private vocabulary, is an allusion to the generals who in 1914 felt sure that a good cavalry charge could sweep through "the much vaunted heavy artillery of the Huns."

A little later I received a visit about which I have often reflected these last few months, because events have given it a new significance. It occurred, if I am not mistaken, during the latter half of the year 1934.

In the meanwhile, though I personally had taken no initiative in the matter, I had become leader of the "July 9th Movement", which united all the youth groups in politics. Many people rightly or wrongly set great store by that movement, or thought it must be reckoned with.

So it happened that Lieutenant-Colonel Didelet, chief of General Weygand's private staff, came to see me. He brought me an article he had just published in the *Revue Hebdomadaire*. He informed me that he would be delighted if I found time to consider the problem, for "some day I might have a word to say on the subject." The article was devoted to "the new army". It was very well written, and on the surface very reasonably thought out. It is only recently that I have understood what it was aiming at. It was in 1934 that Charles de Gaulle's now famous book was published. Like almost everyone else, I had not yet heard of the book. But it had not been unnoticed in military circles. The article written by Lieutenant-Colonel Didelet, close collaborator with Weygand, was entirely directed—as I realized lately on reading de Gaulle's book—against de Gaulle's ideas; and its purpose was to point out to public opinion the danger of creating a professional army, composed mostly of specialists, which would fight in independent units, possessing, for that purpose, powerful, highly perfected equipment.

I am unable to answer the question of when I first met Gamelin at all precisely; probably at some official luncheon or dinner. And for a time I continued to meet him only at official dinners or luncheons.

He had now become in his turn the generalissimo designate. As the threat of war kept growing all around us, anyone as passionately interested as I was in questions of war and peace could not but look with avid curiosity at the man on whom some day all our separate destinies might suddenly depend. Besides I had also been told, by those friends of mine who were now ministers of state, what weight the opinion of the Chief of Staff carries on governmental decisions in moments of crisis. For example, in 1936, when Hitler sent his troops to occupy the Rhineland, the French Cabinet was divided on what attitude France should take. Should we act, or just lie low? A simple technical argument from the Chief of Staff had weighted the scales on the side of inaction: "If you want me to go into the Rhineland, I must have a general mobilization, for I have no expeditionary force and no way of conjuring one up on the spot." The Cabinet hesitated to mobilize five million men for such a simple police job.

A permanent expeditionary corps was just what de Gaulle had called for in his book two years before, showing, with admirable clearness, how through lack of such an instrument France was always condemned to prefer inaction and to watch the destruction of peace, bit by bit, till she would be dragged into a general war under the most unfavourable conditions. But his idea had not been given any attention by the General Staff, nor was the lesson of the Rhineland incident any more useful to them; for when that danger was over, no one heard anything of their hastily trying to put together some plan to create an expeditionary corps, nor did they ever submit such a plan to Parliament, which most certainly would not have rejected it.

For those reasons, every time I saw Gamelin in some official gathering, I watched him with particular attention and always managed to have a short chat with him either before or after the meal.

No man could be less haughty or more pleasant. As

he was always perfectly at ease, he made you feel at ease too, immediately. If you couldn't remember the day you were first introduced to him, it was because from the start he always treated people like old acquaintances. When you shook hands with him, after not having seen him for many months, it seemed as if he had been with you the evening before and you were now resuming a daily conversation. If you were leaving a room at the same time he was, you had to insist before he consented to go first, and his smile would say: "Well, all right—the privilege of age!" Physically, imagine a man of average height and average build, well set up and straight; a fair, pink skin, delicately veined; light eyes, rather hard in colour, perhaps, and without depth of light, a little too much on their guard, but kind and pleasant in their expression; silky, rather sparse hair, ranging in colour from light auburn to fair, and tinged with red. A small, silky moustache. Few wrinkles, or extremely fine ones. An appearance, not exactly of youth, but of excellently preserved health—calm, not at all exuberant health. His voice was pleasant, and he used it to full advantage. He spoke well, in measured and persuasive tones, and did not listen to his own voice. He was an admirable listener; he never interrupted, managed never to contradict. And you felt right away that you wanted to agree with a man whose authority contained so little that was offensive. But there was a kind of magic in it, and in the end you couldn't tell whether your arguments had satisfied him or whether in some subtle way he had succeeded in convincing you.

I asked him one day what was the state of preparation of the German army.

"They are making enormous efforts," he answered, "which are certainly obtaining results. But there is one gap they'll find it hard to fill: the lack of training in those classes corresponding to the period between the liquidation of the old army and the re-establishment of conscription."

He also spoke of the shortage of trained officers which handicapped the Germans, especially of non-commissioned officers and officers in the lower ranks, who cannot be conjured up out of nothing. He also thought that there was a disruption in the tradition of the higher ranks and of the General Staff, and that the upheaval brought into the army by political pre-occupations had only accentuated this.

"I can think of very few of their present generals who fought in responsible posts in 1914-18. Here we are almost all former 1918 division commanders." He gave the names of several of his colleagues. "An experience which it is difficult to replace."

When aviation was mentioned, he dismissed the subject in a few brief words, saying that in France it was now in a period of transition and that we needed to make haste; he insinuated that, after all, he was not responsible for that: "If mistakes have been made and negligence tolerated," he seemed to say, "it has nothing to do with me."

He never gave any details about the equipment of the army itself. But he appeared satisfied and his very discretion was reassuring. In no instance did I see an expression, sense a reticence, hear a sigh, that could be interpreted thus: "I'd have a lot to say—but . . ." or: "You, who can reach both public opinion and the ministers, go and hammer into their ears that I haven't the material I need, that we must make colossal and urgent efforts; otherwise we're headed straight for catastrophe . . ."

He was absolutely unassuming. He seldom spoke of himself or of his past. Others spoke of him instead, and generally in terms of high praise. He had been, it was said, from the very start of the last war, one of the least conspicuous but most efficient of Joffre's assistants; one of those whom Joffre, who was rather touchy and jealous of his authority, preferred because of their personal modesty. The story was told of how Gamelin, having written it out in his own hand, prompted Joffre to give the order that launched the Battle of the Marne. All his career during the World War bore the same mark: adaptability, discretion, efficiency.

I may as well admit now that I had Gamelin in mind when in my *Verdun* I traced the silhouette of Lieutenant-Colonel G. But I did not attempt to draw a portrait, nor did I tie myself down to exact details of biography. The resemblance lies rather in his moral attitude and psychology, and besides contains nothing detrimental to the man in question.

During 1938, a year abundant in danger signals for those who governed France, I had numerous opportunities to discuss Gamelin with them.

"What does Gamelin think of it?" I often asked.

I was told of two particularly dramatic sessions which took place, one during the May crisis, the other just before Munich. The only people present at those sessions formed around Daladier a real war Cabinet, as yet unofficial; they were the Ministers of National Defence and Foreign Affairs, and the heads of the army, navy, and air force—Gamelin, Darlan, and Vuillemin, respectively—summoned there to answer the supremely important question: "Suppose France were obliged to fight tomorrow—could she do it?" Which in other words signified: "Are we in a position to say no if necessary—or must we, eventually, capitulate?" In May, Darlan answered that the navy was in as good shape as could reasonably be expected, and that, supported by the British fleet, we need fear nothing on the seas. That was true. He repeated it in September.

Vuillemin (whom Göring had invited to Berlin some time earlier, not to deceive him about the state of preparedness of the German air force, but, on the contrary, to "take the wind out of his sails", so to speak, by showing him everything) threw his arms out in a hopeless gesture and said: "After two weeks of war we shan't have a single plane left." He was not more cheerful in September. He even added a precise and heart-breaking detail: "At first we'll have to send out our reservists only, because they'll be shot down and we must hold back our good pilots until we get good planes." (And some people still express surprise that in 1938 the French government showed so little enthusiasm for war.)

As for Gamelin, in September, just as in May, he declared, without so much as a glance at the two others, and with a smile full of hidden meaning: "The army is ready."

When we were discussing the situation one day, I said to Georges Bonnet: "But, after all, suppose we're forced into war—what are we going to do? It's all very well to have a thoroughly prepared army, even if we have no air force. But we can't hurl it against the Siegfried Line! Then what? We ought to have a plan. . . . Do you think Gamelin has a plan?"

"So we hear."

That's all I learned about it; and I'm not sure that Bonnet knew anything more definite than that. Gamelin and Daladier had equal rights to the title of "the Silent." There was no proof that the generalissimo took even Daladier into his confidence.

Personally, I thought Gamelin's plan consisted perhaps in taking advantage of the Rome-Berlin Axis, so noisily advertised in both capitals, by definitely linking Italy's fate to Germany's and, in the event of war, launching a vigorous attack on Italy, so striking at Germany from the flank. Bonnet, it is true, when I made some allusion to this, answered: "Your hypothesis might have worked in May. But this is mid-September, and they say the Alpine passes are already blocked."

The problem as stated above: "Suppose we had to march against Germany, how should we do it and on what front?" and its inevitable corollary: "Should we not turn the Italo-German collusion to our advantage?" was a familiar one to all well-informed and thoughtful minds.

I can recall an afternoon in the autumn of 1938. I was strolling along the sidewalk of the Quai d'Orsay with President Herriot.

"We all like Italy well enough," he said. "But those who imagine we can get around her by bowing before her are dangerously naïve. I tried everything when I was in power, all to no purpose. Moreover, in case of conflict with Germany, the worst trick Italy could play on us would be to declare her neutrality. It would be one grave concern out of Germany's way. Italy is the vulnerable part of the Axis, and a hostage we must guard carefully."

"And," I answered, "Italian opinion, which is worth more than the government's, should be kept sufficiently aware of this. Is our General Staff fully conscious of that fact? I don't feel that in Corsica, for example, our preparations are very impressive."

Herriot pouted, nodded:

"Gamelin, you know, does not err in the direction of excessive temerity. In fact I'm afraid he is rather timorous."

It was the first time I heard this stated so clearly, and by someone whose word carried so much weight. I often meditated over it afterwards, and more than once with anxiety.

In August 1939 I spent the last week before war was declared in the closest contact with the government. We all hoped we could still preserve the peace, and Georges Bonnet stuck to the job with particular persistence. But, alas, our hopes steadily declined. Our problem therefore had to be stated more and more in military terms, and "What does Gamelin think?" came up more often than ever. They answered:

"He is not worried about the army . . . but evidently quite concerned over the condition of the air force—we won't be up to the mark in that department until some time in November. . . . He hopes that the German air force won't upset his mobilization too much. Luckily for the D.C.A. (anti-aircraft defence), we've just received the material we needed."

On the morning of August 26—a date I shall never forget (it was also my birthday)—I received from an important foreign statesman who was passing through Paris the request for an interview "about a matter of the utmost urgency".

This man was definitely one of the two or three most powerful political minds that it has been my lot to meet. I shall not state his name, for certain reasons, making here an exception to my rule of saying everything. I asked him to come immediately. He said:

"I need not tell a man like you how serious the situation is. In my opinion, the war is a matter of days. I am very much afraid for France and England. They give the impression that they are going into this war as if it were an unpleasant and terribly boring job, but with no anxiety as to the outcome. That is an enormous mistake. You're not going to win this war without imagination, audacity, creative power. If all you do is to dodge all risk and take the line of least resistance, you'll lose your fight before it even begins, and the consequences will be terrible. . . . Now listen: You are influential with your government. Go and say this to Daladier, to Bonnet: Mussolini, who is not very intelligent, but the craftiest of actors, is going to play a terrible trick on you. He'll lie low just long enough. He'll let you hope for his neutrality. He'll even make you pay for it. That's the best help he can give Germany, by furnishing her with fresh supplies and protecting all her southern flank. He'll declare war against you just a fortnight before Hitler's victory is assured—to have his share of the loot. . . ." (As a matter of fact, Mussolini showed even greater caution.)

"Your government," he continued, "must send the following statement to Mussolini immediately: 'We give you forty-eight hours to reach a decision, with us or against us.' Mussolini wants to avoid war at all costs just now. He lately received disastrous reports on the state of his air force and artillery, about which he knew little. Public opinion in Italy is opposed to war. . . . If Mussolini tries to evade the question by a promise of neutrality, exact from him the permission to occupy Turin, Milan, and two or three other towns, as a guarantee, and the right of passage for your troops. If he threatens to declare war on you, send an appeal to the Italian nation. Tell them the truth . . . reassure them with regard to your intentions. Within a fortnight Mussolini will be over-thrown, and Italy will go to war against Germany, on your side, delighted to break free of an alliance she detests and to rehabilitate herself. But if you flatter Mussolini—all is lost."

Then he went on: "It is your government you must convince first. The English are rather stupid and Churchill is not in power. They'll understand later. . . . Your government of course will want to consult the General Staff. Absurd! Staff officers are just servants of the state. I once governed my country, and I know them. Like all civil servants they are afraid of complications and always seek a minimum of responsibility. They are mere tools. They are created to obey. If you ask for their advice in a manœuvre of this kind, they'll all say; 'No, no! There's quite enough to fuss over as things are!" The question to ask them is not 'Should we do this?' but 'How will you carry out this operation when we give you the order to do it?' "

I answered: "Your suggestion is of capital importance. You develop it so forcefully that they must hear it directly from your own lips, not through me. I'll see that the necessary interview takes place. I'll be there to support you."

The interview took place on the next day, a Sunday, in my apartment (and not in an official building, to evade the vigilance of spies). My statesman was as eloquent and persuasive as before. He left a strong impression.

On Monday I took a letter to Georges Bonnet, addressed to him but, in point of fact, destined for Daladier; in it, recalling the interview of the day before, I said that not to take into account the warning of this man, whose words we had all too often failed to heed in the past, was to assume a heavy responsibility.

I waited. Then I was told that the Premier was thinking it over . . . that after all it was a matter on which no decision could be made without the General Staff. . . .

The declaration of war came, and the time to place our troops. Nothing more was said. Anyway it was too late.

One day I said to Bonnet (who had just shifted to the Ministry of Justice from the Ministry of Foreign Affairs, which had been taken over by Daladier): "Well, what happened to our affair—you know, putting Mussolini on the spot?"

"Gamelin was opposed to it. He said: 'All I need is a fortnight to complete my mobilization in peace. Even if Italy starts to attack immediately after that first fortnight, I'd rather that than have her jump on us right away.'"

I went to see Coulondre, who was acting as minister at the Quai d'Orsay. He confirmed the statement that Gamelin had asked to be allowed "to finish his mobilization in peace." "He seems fairly pleased that the Germans haven't done anything to bother him since September 3."

Coulondre added:

"And now,—just to reassure you on the subject of Italy—ah, if I could tell you!—you'd be terribly surprised—well, I'll tell you just the same: they're providing us with bombing planes. Superb Capronis—see?"

I was amused, but not quite without misgivings. Some time later my friend Erik Labonne, Resident General in Tunisia, who was passing through Paris, said gaily: "You've heard about the Capronis? Grand! They won't cost us a cent. You see, I pay for them with my olive oil and phosphates."

As for Gamelin, it was, of course, completely out of the question to try to see him at such a moment. But from all one could hear about him it seemed obvious that his only ambition was to "finish his mobilization in peace," and he just couldn't get over the fact that the Germans were giving him plenty of time, with the most unaccountable consideration.

As I wish to be perfectly fair, I must add that in October I had cause to modify my general impression—the mission which I assumed, to the King of the Belgians, was inspired as much by Gamelin as by Daladier. And as we shall see later, it showed at first both firmness and audacity. But I wonder now if Gamelin did not think of it, essentially, as an added measure of prudence, in accord with his desire of still further limiting the extent of the risk.

On the morning of December 16, 1939 I was called to the telephone. An infinitely courteous voice:

"Hello. Captain Huet speaking, of General Gamelin's personal staff. . . . Allow me to present my respects. . . . General Gamelin expects you today, any time after five thirty p. m."

"Any time after—I'm not sure I understand."

"Yes—at any time convenient to you, *Maître*, after five thirty p.m. We will send a car from General Headquarters to get you some twenty minutes beforehand."

The ministers with whom I was most intimate did not leave me as much latitude when I made appointments with them. That the time of the generalissimo, chief commander of the Allied armies, should thus be left at my disposal rather took my breath away.

"I should prefer," said I, "that the general should indicate the time most convenient for him."

"Certainly not, *Maître*, the choice is yours."

"Well," I said, somewhat at random, "at a quarter to six."

"Right. The car will be at your door at a quarter past five. My respects. . . ."

I had sent word to Gamelin, a few days before, that I should like to visit the front. I wished to find out, at first hand, what this "phony war" was like, and how our troops were taking it. I had also said I should be pleased to pay my respects to the general before leaving, if he had a moment to spare, but that I should understand perfectly if he could find no time to see me.

At a quarter past five the car was at my door, a large black Renault limousine. The soldier in charge, looking very neat, in fact almost elegant, opened the door. We drove rapidly through the Parisian blackout.

At first I recognized the road without difficulty, in spite of the darkness, punctuated only by anonymous lights. I supposed we were going to Vincennes; besides I am very familiar with the roads in Paris and in its immediate outskirts. But after a certain point I began to lose all sense of direction. The car would suddenly swing to the left, or the right, and take inexplicable detours. The drive was lasting longer than it should, according to the time we were making, for I could see that the hand on the luminous dial seldom went below forty miles. "Am I being taken somewhere else, and not to Vincennes?" I wondered. "Or have the chauffeurs orders to confuse the visitors they bring along?"

Then came a road between rows of trees, the noise

of the wheels stopping on gravel. The chauffeur opened the door. I got out in front of a very sombre building; in the darkness I could distinguish neither its length nor its height; only one square of light cut the darkness—a door with two or three steps in front of it.

Without a question a guard showed me into a fairly large, low-ceilinged room, a very depressing, very badly lighted room, furnished most lamentably—a table strewn with military periodicals, and a few odd chairs, all strongly reminiscent of barracks. There was no one there. The whole surrounding atmosphere was strangely calm; no coming and going, no sound of arrivals at the door, no trace of any visitors. On a Saturday, in the early evening, at the headquarters of the general-in-chief—how very fantastic! Just imagine the waiting-room of the least important minister of state, or even of a prefect at the same moment. . . . I had no time for further observations, for a young officer appeared.

"Monsieur Jules Romains?"

"Yes, captain."

"My respects, *Maître*. I shall notify the general of your presence."

He came back almost instantly.

"Kindly follow me, please."

As I followed him I resolved not to take advantage

of the general's courtesy, and to remain ten minutes at the most.

A door opened into a vast oblong room, brilliantly lighted; a few pillars supported the low ceiling. I saw Gamelin coming towards me, his hand held out, with a happy smile on a face that showed no sign of strain. He wore the very plain uniform of a field-general, with plain beige puttees. In the room I could see several tables, maps on the wall and on the tables, and a few ordinary chairs. General Gamelin was alone.

He asked me to sit down, somewhere, almost in the centre of the room, not far from one of the pillars, and sat opposite me, a couple of paces away, his legs crossed.

And now he began one of the most extraordinary conversations I have ever had in all my life. At the time I was indeed extremely struck by it. But during the catastrophic events of May and June 1940 I thought about it day after day, and each time I have become more and more convinced that it was of exceptional historic value. In it I see the whole mystery of the character who played such a part in the destiny of each one of us (even of the people in this hemisphere), a mystery so strongly lighted as to become more disconcerting than if it were in semi-darkness.

First he made an allusion to my latest journey.

"Just back from Switzerland, I suppose?"

He was amazingly calm, and smiling. He asked me questions on my impressions of Switzerland, on the state of mind among the people, on what I had heard in political circles. He seemed to be very well informed already. He chatted quietly, pleasantly, just as a nobleman in his country château might chat with a friend come to visit him after having been away for some time.

I told him I should be going back to Belgium in a fortnight. He made some remark about my first journey there in October. "I know," he said, "how good a job you did," and went on, recalling one of the problems I had had to submit to the Belgian government.

"Just think that any one of my motorized units, going from one of our frontiers to the other, would stretch out over sixty miles of road. And, after all, there are only two or three roads. . . . What a target for planes!"

We took up the subject of what I had learned in Switzerland about the morale in Germany during that month of December 1939.

"Personally," he observed, "I don't believe there will be a spontaneous collapse of Germany, without a military defeat. I don't think the blockade, and the privations it causes, will have any direct influence. People won't revolt for that reason. What I am more inclined to admit are indirect results: a physiological weakness, produced in the long run by shortage of food, might lower nervous resistance and make the whole nation more easily vulnerable to the first shock received."

As we chatted we touched on all aspects of the international situation. Everything Gamelin said was measured and carefully thought out. He seemed to have full information on every point. And I, who knew the countries we were discussing and was constantly receiving information from them, could only admire the surprising accuracy of judgment the general showed in his opinions on foreign affairs. Now I no longer felt as if he were a provincial nobleman, but rather a prodigiously well-informed historian of contemporary events.

I brought the conversation around to the first days of the war. Certain things still rankled in my mind. When I made some allusion to Italy, Gamelin remarked: "Oh, if I'd had to pitch into the Italians, I'd have done things differently. . . ."

But he never explained why he had not wanted to "pitch into the Italians", or even threaten that he would. "Differently" meant "not as I did on the Lorraine front."

We spoke next of the withdrawal of our troops on the Lorraine front at the beginning of October. I took the liberty to say that it had been a mistake to make so much of the slight advance during the first weeks, and to allow the word to be spread almost officially that Saarbrücken was taken; so that consequently the retreat, when it came, gave a very bad impression in foreign countries. He said he agreed with me completely, but that he had nothing to do with any blunders in information. And he remarked, concerning that first advance:

"Just the same, I succeeded at the time in diverting forty-five German divisions, and that might have been a help to Poland."

I took the opportunity of asking him what he thought of the Polish campaign, and he answered with a disillusioned smile:

"When Marshal Rydz-Smigly came here a few months ago, I pointed out to him the great importance of establishing, along their western front, a fortified line, as continuous as possible. He said: 'Oh, I have an army of manœuvre.'" A short laugh shook Gamelin. "As if I didn't have an army of manœuvre too!"

Then we talked about the Finnish war, which had just broken out, but in which Finnish resistance was already asserting itself in the most impressive way.

"You see," he observed, "with their Mannerheim Line, they've stalled the Russian advance. I know that the Russians aren't the Germans, but then, the Mannerheim Line is not the Maginot Line."

Then we spoke of the Maginot Line, of the protection it had afforded the mobilization and arrangement of our troops. It was chiefly because of the line, Gamelin was convinced, that the offensive had not yet been launched on the western front by the Germans; a flanking attack, through Belgium and Holland, required vast preparation, and the enemy could not organize it in detail while busy in Poland.

"And that gave us a little welcome breathing-space," said Gamelin. "It was very lucky for us. I've had the Maginot Line reinforced; we may say that at present it has doubled its power of resistance, and that was done since this time last year. I've had it extended towards the north, along the Belgian frontier."

"But—with field fortifications?—or something strong enough?"

"Already serious fortifications, which we now know how to build in reinforced concrete with very rapid modern methods. Yes. . . . I'm very glad you're going to take a look at it all. They won't have time to show you everything, but just the same you'll get an idea."

I admitted that I was very curious indeed to visit the front, to go as far as possible into the first lines, and to see the so peculiar war that was going on there.

"Yes," he replied, tilting his head back slightly in a meditative attitude, "this kind of war is indeed quite different from anything we have experienced before. First, because there is no more question of waging a little war every day, as in 1914—attacks on trenches, sudden assaults, useless exchange of artillery fire, general waste of human lives—all that is over on both sides. . . . But, moreover, it is the whole nature of the war that is profoundly new. Very few people realize it . . . or they don't go beyond judging this stagnant war as something incomprehensible. . . . You know, the kind of people who always think the last war is going to start over again—the everlasting error. . . ." He smiled. "This war and the last have nothing in common."

He seemed lost in thought for a moment.

"No one seems to realize that the war of 1914 itself was an exception, a kind of monstrosity; but if we look back through history—for example, the eighteenth century had its stagnant wars, in which nothing occurred for months. You laid siege to a fortified town, indefinitely. You established winter quarters. Then, one fine day, there was a battle. It didn't last long, but it was decisive."

His luminous eyes, staring at the ceiling, expressed all the serenity of a thinker accustomed to dominating events. He reminded me now of my illustrious neighbour Henri Bergson, who, when I went to see him in his country home, sometimes would think aloud before me.

Gamelin, too, was now thinking aloud. And he seemed to enjoy it. I did all I could to encourage him, mostly by proving that I was following him carefully. Besides, as I had noticed on other occasions, and as some allusion made by Gamelin indicated, the generals of this war had read my *Verdun*, published the year before; and in their opinion the man who could write, were it only the first fifty pages, was no rank amateur. They could take the trouble of mentioning a number of things in his presence, certain that they were not wasted on him.

And now I came to asking him how he foresaw future developments of the war.

"To understand just what is happening," he answered, his eyes still fixed on the ceiling, "and what is going to happen, it must be clear that the armies themselves have undergone a change in nature. They have become instruments of great value, in which a tremendous quantity of power has been accumulated . . . very expensive to build and to maintain . . . very highly efficient . . . but insatiably voracious. The uninitiated have no idea of what can be consumed, in a single day's battle, in the way of munitions and fuel. . . . You see, the present state of our armies might be compared to that of the fleets at the time of the last war. A fleet was then indeed a very valuable thing, a very intricate mechanism of enormous power which one tried to keep intact as long as possible, and risked only at the last minute, in a short decisive action."

I was passionately attentive. Nowhere yet had I heard such new and forceful ideas on the present war. He lowered his voice a little, almost confidentially.

"You want to know how I imagine the near future? Well, I think that a period of apparently complete immobility will be followed abruptly by an action into which every resource will be flung all at once"—he bent his head a little and frowned—"and in which the decision will come much more rapidly than people think." His voice deepened, became almost gloomy; he was looking straight in front of him. "Yes, it will be very rapid—and terrible. People don't imagine how terrible it will be!"

Referring again to my coming trip to Belgium, I asked if he did not think that the action he had just described in such an impressive way would come from that direction.

"Very probably," he said, "though it also is wiser to foresee that an attempt might be made by the enemy to submerge the separate invasion of Holland and Belgium in a general thrust forward from the estuary of the Rhine to the Swiss frontier."

"And when do you think such a thrust will come?"

He thought again, bit his lip.

"The end of January isn't out of the question. But I hardly think so. . . . March, a good deal more probable. . . ." Then, after further searching: "May —yes, May, almost certainly." I was struck by such amazing predictions, so calmly pronounced. General Gamelin seemed to envisage the future, if not with a a light heart, at least without terror. I remarked that the respite which he anticipated gave room to hope that by then we should have made up our deficiencies, and more specifically with regard to our aviation.

"Yes," he said in a steady voice, but with an imperceptible trace of reticence. "By March we'll just about come up to the mark."

"As far as tanks are concerned," I went on, "the Belgians tell me they have the best existing anti-tank guns."

"True."

The clock on the wall, at which I glanced every now and then, indicated that I had been there for one hour and ten minutes. I felt some alarm. Several times in my conversation with the general I hinted that I had scruples about taking up so much of his time; but in each instance he answered, with a little wave of his hand: "Not at all, not at all, you are not disturbing me in the least."

During one hour and ten minutes not once did the telephone ring, not once did a collaborator appear. There was not so much as a knock on the door. Truly an atmosphere of unbelievable serenity.

At last I rose. He said:

"I'm going to show you a cross-section of the army." He smiled. "You began this evening with me; you'll go on to General Headquarters; then you'll visit a general in command of a group of armies; next a general at the head of an army; then one of the main forts of the Maginot Line, and as far as possible through to the outposts. . . . On your way you're fairly sure to meet a few generals . . . a few colonels. . . . Keep your eyes open." He smiled once more. "Of course all that you are shown must remain strictly confidential. . . . When you return I shall consider it a pleasure to talk it over with you."

This is no place to give an account of my journey to the armies, although I found it of intense interest. And indeed I observed a great many things. The evening of my return, December 24, I judged it preferable, in keeping with a method I have often applied, to begin by sending General Gamelin a short written report, rather than asking him immediately for an interview—and making it clear that I should like to see him. Needless to say, I was careful in my report to avoid the ridiculousness of showing off any military competence, and presented, or rather insinuated, my remarks with all possible discretion and under cover of carefully chosen circumlocutions. Nevertheless it was clear that I had observed serious deficiencies and was taking the liberty of bringing them to the attention of the man who, in the whole world, was best fitted to remedy them.

For instance, I said of the first lines:

"One feels surprised at the scarcity of bomb-proof shelters, at the complete absence of trenches which might serve as shelters in case of bombing. Officers, questioned by me on what they did in case of bombing, answered that they merely scattered the men in the woods and advised them to lie flat in holes or ordinary hollow spaces in the ground. . . ."

About the Maginot Line itself:

"On examining the outer defences, an incompetent but attentive visitor finds them less impressive than he had expected, though they were, it is said, but recently completed. The anti-tank traps appear somewhat economical; there are a few ditches; the barbed-wire entanglements are certainly not negligible, but they have less depth and are not so long as one would like to imagine *a priori*."

And about the main forts in the line:

"This is perhaps a suitable place to indicate, with all due reservations, an impression, probably based on very slight evidence, but which the uninitiated visitor cannot help receiving, that to the enormous and invulnerable mass of concrete constructions most marvellously planned inside, there corresponds a firing capacity that seems to have been set at the lowest indispensable requirement. And though one is persuaded that such perfectly protected and well-served guns are incomparably superior in efficiency

76

to field-guns, one cannot imagine without difficulty how, in the event of a violent and massive drive by the enemy, they could manage to cover with sufficient density the considerable space which it is their business to make impregnable both in front and on their flanks. . . ."

I also mentioned the serious complaints gathered from the lips of army generals on the subject of the air force, and the danger which I thought I saw in the excessive tranquillity of army life just behind the front lines. It was not difficult for a mind as far-seeing as Gamelin's to seize the full significance of my remarks, in spite of the extreme politeness in which I had made it a point to envelop them.

He did not answer, nor send for me. And I never saw him again.

To begin with, I must declare very humbly that I do not flatter myself that I can throw complete light on this very singular case, which probably reaches into obscurities basic in human nature. But I shall try to disinguish something.

One thing is certain at the outset: those who say and repeat, since the catastrophe, that Gamelin was an imbecile, a "Colonel Blimp," only prove that they themselves don't know what they're talking about. When Paul Reynaud, last May, said that what was missing was an intellectual effort, and that it was time to "think the war," his remarks, aimed at Gamelin, whom he was about to replace, fell wide of the mark. The man who sat opposite me in December 1939 and said the things I have quoted possessed without doubt a very luminous mind, a mind which did not function in a vacuum, but applied itself directly to the problems of war, and in their most recent developments. The predictions he made before me then have since revealed the mark of a really prodigious lucidity. It is impossible to read them over without a kind of shudder.

Then there are those who say: "Gamelin succeeded in his career thanks to the politicians whom he flattered." To begin with, they forget that army men, if they are to reach the highest grades, are always obliged to reckon with politicians, and more or less to win their favour. But that is no argument either for or against their military worth. It must be remembered that young Bonaparte succeeded, thanks to his cleverness in managing politicians. And were not the victorious generals of the Third Reich also made by politics? But we can carry the argument further and hold, without paradox, that it is excellent that politicians, who are civilians and not army men, should decide whom to promote to the highest ranks in the army. For army men would much more surely place obstacles in the way of independent talent, and even more in the way of genius. Was it politicians or army men who silenced Charles de Gaulle?

It is none the less evident, you will say, that the man who with extraordinary lucidity predicted as if by magic the events of May allowed the armies he commanded to become an almost passive prey to those events. It is also evident, if we consider a minute but highly significant fact, that he expressed his confidence and esteem by sharing with me his highest thoughts in an interview lasting more than an hour; but I offended him by pointing out, although with the most prudent politeness, that everything at the front was not exactly perfect.

To be sure—and that is precisely what brings us nearer the truth. He must certainly be one of those men of vast and keen intelligence who do not like to be disturbed in their conception of things. I may add that they avoid any circumstances which might oblige them to change that conception. I was told that he did not often go to the front or even to the military zone; that almost all his journeys as commander-in-chief of the Allied armies were either between the Castle of Vincennes and Daladier's office, rue Saint-Dominique, or between Vincennes and London, when the Supreme Council of War was held there. And it was certainly not the fear of danger which held him back (nor fatigue, I was about to add, but that is not certain). It was more probably desire to avoid fuss and complications, disagreeable discoveries he might make, punishments he would have to hand out, and incidents about which anger would have to be shown. He preferred to "think the war"—like Descartes in his *poêle*.

He was one of those, I suppose, whose intellectual forces are badly co-ordinated with their forces of action. Between the two the current passes not at all or but faintly. What causes this leak in transmission? First of all, an essential lack of will; such people do not *will* with force and effectiveness what they think. But it is due also to a peculiar fear of action itself and the consequences created by it. (Just remember Herriot's words about Gamelin and imagine how this tendency would be accentuated by the red tape and routine inherent in the General Staff.)

Such men are fundamentally dreamers. And it is common knowledge that a dreamer attains prodigious lucidity, even in matters of everyday life.

A dreamer, if he is an architect, for instance, dreams of admirable buildings he would like to construct, and sees every detail; but he overlooks one last detail—trivial, indeed, but rich in unexpected and irksome difficulties—he must build it.

What is rarer, and consequently less open to suspicion, is that a dreamer of this type should be generalissimo of the French armies, commander-in-chief of the Allied armies; that he should dream of tanks, unconcerned by the fact that few tanks were available; and dream of an absorbingly interesting blitz-krieg, which would take place in May, yet do nothing, or very little, to assure victory for himself rather than for the other fellow.

III

THE MYSTERY OF LEOPOLD III

EARLY ON the morning of Saturday, December 24, 1938, Christmas Eve, I was called to the telephone by a friend of mine who has nothing to do with politics, a painter, who is also a passionate friend of peace. (He has devoted some admirable drawings to the desecration of the idol of war.)

"X asked me to call you up," he said. "He didn't know your phone number. He'd very much like to see you."

"So? He's here? Why, yes, of course, with pleasure. But I've a certain number of appointments. . . . Is it urgent?"

"It couldn't be more urgent, I'm told."

"H'm—m! What's it about, do you know?"

"Not the vaguest idea."

"Well, tell him to give me a ring—I shan't budge an inch all morning. We'll make an appointment."

A few minutes later X's harsh but quite cordial voice came to me over the phone.

"I'm here in Paris on purpose to see you," he said. "I have very little time at my disposal."

"Are you free around noon? Come and have lunch with me?"

"Fine. Thank you. But—don't mind my asking—we'll be alone?"

"Quite. Just my wife and the servants. . . ." I sensed some reticence at the other end of the line. "Listen, we have lunch at one. Come here at twelve or a quarter to twelve. We'll talk in complete privacy."

"Right."

I reflected that if X, a man neither frivolous nor inclined to agitation—indeed, quite the contrary—had come to Paris on purpose to see me, and surrounded by so many precautions, the affair must be serious.

I warned the maid:

"Around noon a gentleman will come to see me. You are not to ask him for his name. Just say: 'You are the gentleman Monsieur Romains is expecting?'"

Shortly before noon X walked into my study in the Faubourg Saint-Honoré.

It was good to see him again—a tall, strapping fellow with a very ruddy, rustic face; a distinct voice with a strong tang of the soil, having to search for his words sometimes, but then pronouncing them with vigour. A man little given to empty phrases, who stuck fast to reality.

"Please excuse all this mystery," he began, "but the interest at stake is considerable, and absolute secrecy is necessary."

"Don't worry. No one except my wife will so much as know I saw you. And I can vouch for her discretion."

"I'm here, really, sent by the King." He thought an instant, his head bent, staring at a corner of the room. "Yes, it's something great; it will be very great if it succeeds; great enough, I think, to kindle the enthusiasm of a man like you."

"You're making me terribly curious."

"King Leopold—you know his special channels of information—has just received warning from Berlin—of a very disturbing kind. The King feels that the danger is rapidly growing, and that we'll soon be on the well-soaped slope which leads to disaster."

"Ah! I'm not far from thinking that myself. The respite Munich procured lasted so short a time."

"Then you're in the right mood to hear me." He looked straight into my eyes. "For you haven't changed, have you? You're still a 'Man of Good Will'?"

I must explain here that X was one of the members

of a kind of order of chivalry which was recruited little by little throughout Europe; a completely ideal order, alas, without a constitution, without a recognized leader, without regulations. Every one of these men had made for himself more or less the same vow as I had in the past: to work at preserving peace in the world; and all believed as I did in the method of personal action on *vital points*. The name "Men of Good Will" they sometimes used for themselves, half seriously, half jokingly. They were in sympathy though far apart; they tried to work in the same direction; they sent emissaries to one another; occasionally they met and lent one another a hand. But it's a great pity they never constituted a real order, like those in the past. For they might then really have preserved peace in the world.

I answered: "I haven't changed."

"I felt sure of that. . . . Well, we can even give the precise date on which we'll reach our well-soaped slope. You know about the trip Chamberlain and Halifax will take to Rome in mid-January. This Chamberlain is a candid old man. . . . King Leopold, thanks to his connections with the Italian royal family, is fairly well informed in what concerns Rome. He has reasons to think the interview will come to nothing, and that immediately afterwards the rhythm of events will become accelerated. . . . Now look! You know the five we call the 'sovereigns of the Oslo

Conference'—the King of Sweden, the King of Norway, the King of Denmark, the Queen of the Netherlands, and King Leopold himself. They have remained in close contact, and have also kept a certain prestige in the eyes of Europe and America, just because of this conference. . . . Now, here is King Leopold's plan: four of them will write, at almost the same time, to the fifth—they'll agree which it is to be—a very solemn, very moving letter, most human in its tone, in which they will beseech him to do something in the name of them all to save Europe from imminent war and establish a lasting peace. The fifth will immediately send a letter, itself very solemn and very pathetic, in the name of all five, to each of the four men on whom the peace of Europe now depends—Chamberlain, Daladier, Hitler, and Mussolini. He will say that it is to them that the nations look for an end to their intolerable anguish; and he will ask them to call, as soon as possible, a large conference, in which all the problems of Europe, military, territorial, economic, colonial, would be discussed and resolved. His letter, with those of the four other sovereigns which preceded it, will be brought, the same day, to the knowledge of the whole world. . . ."

"Yes, yes—I see, perfectly. . . ."

"You understand—the King is staking his chance on three elements of success: secrecy beforehand, rapidity, and a dramatic quality. The opinion of nations still exists. But we can't act on it as before. We live in a time of movies and radio, of vast publicity, of spectacular, monster meetings. To exercise pressure on rulers or to encourage them in any one direction, the slow action of spreading ideas is no longer sufficient. An effect of shock must be produced on the sensibility and imagination of the masses. . . . I needn't say that to you, who have repeated it so often. . . . But a shock, to reach its maximum effect, must be unexpected, and nothing must deaden it beforehand. If a thing is prepared long ahead by chancellery notes, by an exchange of views in which everyone has his say and puts on the brakes a little, and at the same time is reported by the press—then when at last it happens, all its effect is discounted already, its impetus lost. Nobody is interested, nobody believes in it. . . . The King wishes to act in secret and quickly. He hasn't told his government, not even M. Spaak. Our Ambassador in Paris knows nothing either, and will know nothing. The thing will fall like a thunderbolt. At present only three people are in on it: the King, myself, and, in the last five minutes, you."

I listened with emotion, overcome by enthusiasm. Yes, that was really a great idea. Had it come to the young King spontaneously, or had X prompted it? No matter—anyway it was a credit to them both. And it was a great opportunity, one such as I had dreamed of in the past, without daring to hope for its realization;

almost more romantic than those I had imagined in my novel. . . . To conspire with a king, and soon with five kings, to preserve peace in the world! For I felt sure something was going to be asked of me.

I told X that the plan was a fine one, and, besides, very reasonable—like all bold ideas rejected by mediocre minds because they upset the meanness of their imagination. "Nothing of that type has yet been attempted," I insisted. "It will be new and thrilling. If anything can still succeed, it is the very thing that will succeed."

"And all the more," X went on, "because we are sure of a powerful echo in America and throughout the Catholic world. It wouldn't be surprising if the Pope and Mr. Roosevelt felt impelled then to join their voices to the others. . . ."

"But don't the other four sovereigns know yet?"

"No, as I told you."

"Are you sure of their adherence?"

"It is morally certain."

"But—to obtain it, you'll have to broaden the secret a little?"

"Only just so far as is absolutely necessary. I'm taking the matter in hand myself. Everything will go through the most rapid and confidential channels."

"So—the other four will write to King Leopold?"

"He doesn't insist on that; on the contrary. He thinks we ought to choose Queen Wilhelmina, for various reasons; or, failing that, the King of Sweden. But if no one else takes on the job, he won't evade it. . . . I'm not worried about that. But there's another problem. We're enthusiastic men, but we're not children; we don't want to go headlong into failure, which would itself be spectacular. . . . So we're obliged beforehand to sound out the four recipients—Chamberlain, Daladier, Hitler, Mussolini."

"But then—aren't you afraid of falling back into the methods you're trying to avoid?"

"There's no connection. The chancelleries will be left out. And in direct contacts, obtained without delay, we'll ask the four in question to give their word of honour that they themselves will keep the thing secret, till the last minute. Why not?"

"H'm . . . quite likely. Such an unwonted procedure may strike them. . . ."

"As for the substance of the affair, all we'll ask each of them is: 'Are you disposed to receive such a letter, and to take it into account?' Each one, questioned thus and without witnesses, will be freer to answer. Even Hitler and Mussolini aren't going to war with a light heart, but they're afraid to lose face . . . or to look as if they were making advances to their adversary."

"Right," said I, looking at him with a smile. "And so—?"

"So—you said it was a great idea? Well? Secure France's yes as the first."

I thought it over.

"You want me to take you to Daladier?"

He thought in his turn, and shook his head.

"Is that necessary? I'd have to give my name to the usher. . . . People who know me might catch sight of me. They'd speculate. . . . You could explain it all to him with less fuss, in a tête-á-tête. All that matters is that I should leave with an answer, Monday afternoon at the latest. . . . You need only say: 'All set. Go ahead.' That'll be enough for me—and for the King."

I turned it over in my mind.

"Listen. I'm willing to ask Daladier for an appointment immediately. But I'm sure he'll undertake nothing without consulting his Minister of Foreign Affairs . . . and then Georges Bonnet, considering on what close terms we are, will be astonished that I didn't speak to him first . . . while the other way around he'd be a precious ally. . . . By the time I presented myself at Daladier's, Georges Bonnet, I hope, would already have convinced him."

"Do what's best. . . . I'd like as few as possible in the secret. Remember, Spaak knows nothing! Well, you vouch for Georges Bonnet. . . . I'll tell you at what times I'll be without fail at my hotel. As soon as you know anything, telephone. Watch your words,

though. . . . I'll hop right over here, or elsewhere.
. . . In short, I'll be on the lookout."

Thereupon we went into the drawing-room for
cocktails, most casually. And X, true to his Flemish
blood, spoke with competence about the pictures
hanging on the walls.

I had said to Georges Bonnet, over the telephone:
"We must be strictly alone, for quite a while."

Told that it was "exceptional in both importance
and urgency," he managed by shifting other appointments to receive me that same afternoon.

As I entered the famous office of the Quai d'Orsay,
with its wooden panelling and gilt, where the fate of
France and of many other nations had so often been
sealed, he said to one of his assistants who was standing near him, some papers in his hand:

"Say that I am not to be disturbed, on any pretext,
until I ring. Take the telephone calls."

The man went out. Bonnet sat in an attitude habit-
ual with him in such cases. He turned his armchair
at an angle, towards me, seated on the other side of
the desk; settled himself squarely in the chair and, his
head bent, fixed his very attentive eyes on me. Having
seen that paper and pencil were within reach, he said,
in his precise and terse tone:

"My dear friend, I am listening."

"What I have come to say must be known to President Daladier and to you only. At present total secrecy must be kept."

"Right." He pushed aside the pencil and paper.

"I take the liberty of insisting, my dear friend, that none of your assistants, even the most intimate among the President's and your own, should have wind of it. I gave my word on that."

"You have mine."

I explained. When I quoted King Leopold's opinion that if we failed to make a supreme effort we should soon be on the way to catastrophe, Bonnet broke in and declared categorically:

"That's just what I think."

When I had finished explaining the set-up, he said, in the voice of a man who, while listening, weighed every word of yours and all his own responsibilities:

"Personally, my answer is yes. France cannot refuse to take part in such an attempt."

"And—you think that President Daladier will agree?"

"I think I can quite positively say yes."

A deep feeling of hope took possession of me. It seemed to me that the portents gathered ominously over the times were dispersing, and that perhaps, thanks to the connivance of a few men of good will, the destiny of Europe was about to turn suddenly, with an ease that would surprise us later. For there is a slope towards good as towards evil. I resumed:

"Do you see any reservations we should make? Any subjects we shouldn't wish to be touched upon at the conference?"

"No. I don't think that's a good method. Any reservations we make will suggest others to our good neighbours, and then the whole conference will be emptied of its substance. If we want to arrive at a lasting solution and establish peace, then, on the contrary, all questions must be discussed freely, every abscess drained."

"Even the question of the limitation of armaments?"

"Certainly. On that point, say, if you like, that, without making formal reservation, we very much hope that the conference will take some account of programs in course of execution."

I went on:

"So far as I'm concerned, it would be all right if you gave me Daladier's answer without my hearing it from his own lips; but out of deference towards the King, and considering the exceptional gravity of the affair, it would be better if I could say to his emissary: 'The Premier himself instructed me to say he agrees.' "

"Quite. . . . He is particularly rushed because of his coming journey to Corsica and North Africa, but I'll ask him to summon you by telephone."

On Sunday the 25th, as the Christmas bells rang, I watched the good people of Paris walking along the streets, many with small parcels in their hands. I thought: "They are off to family dinners, they are going to call on one another, give presents. . . . They have no idea that five or six of us are plotting to try to keep peace for them and for their children—the peace they love so much more than they realize!"

Alas! there was some naïveté in my reverie, for it is probable that at the same time others—a handful too —were following on their side a completely different reverie. And the stars had decreed that this time it would not be the Men of Good Will who would triumph. But the stars had decreed something yet more disturbing and incomprehensible: that the figure of the young King, the conspirator for peace, our companion and accomplice in this our sacred task— the figure of the young King, enveloped in such a beautiful light on that Christmas Day of 1938, should appear to us seventeen months later shrouded in the dark veil of betrayal. . . . When did we misjudge him? On December 25, 1938—or on May 28, 1940? It is too early to try to answer.

On Monday the 26th I was able to say to the King's Man (*"l'homme du roi"*):

"You can go, satisfied that you have hit the first mark. France says yes, without reservation."

(I merely mentioned the desire put forward on the subject of armament programs in the course of execution.)

"Well now!" exclaimed the King's Man, his chest expanded by an optimistic laugh, "I'll make short work of the rest!"

As he stood, his tall and robust body seemed ready to clear hedge upon hedge in an obstacle race. He strode up and down in the narrow space of my study.

"You must know all we're going to do, the King and I, so that you can follow our work at a distance, and so that a note from me to you every now and then, in veiled terms, of course, will be sufficient to let you know where we are. . . . I'm going back to Brussels tonight. First thing tomorrow from Brussels I'll ask Neville Chamberlain for an appointment—I'll go to London to see him myself. The King, on his side, will make it his business to prepare an interview with Mussolini in Rome. I hope that'll be easy. . . . Same tactics with regard to Hitler—that'll probably be a bit tougher. . . . In the meantime I'll see the three Premiers of Denmark, Norway, and Sweden—the only men to be taken into our confidence with their sovereigns. I'll do it all by plane. If I can I'll get them all three in the same place—it'll be easier that way. . . . Between two planes, I'll make arrangements with Holland, or the King will see the Queen. . . . To do it properly, by the middle of next week we ought to have everything settled with England so that only Hitler and Mussolini are left. Hitler first, if possible, for if he says yes, Mussolini can't say no . . . but I must succeed in seeing Mussolini before the arrival in Rome of Chamberlain and Halifax—that's before the 12th. . . . Then our scene is set; we let the interview in Rome pass . . . we let the international press groan or speak ironically about its failure; then the 19th or 20th off goes our bomb, eh? By the end of January we'll know what to think."

"And you'll do that alone!" I exclaimed admiringly.

"Oh, the King will help me . . . but you know when you really want something it's the safest way."

"If people begin to put as much dynamics into a good cause as into a bad one, then there's some hope."

I added: "If you foresee any difficulty from Berlin, why don't you try to see Abetz? I have a feeling he too has remained a Man of Good Will and can be trusted."

"True—I hadn't thought of that. A good idea. . . ."

"I'm sorry," I said, "that I'm obliged to leave quite soon for North Africa, where I'll be moving around with no permanent address. . . . My journey was planned a long time ago. . . . It'll be a nuisance."

We made several arrangements concerning our correspondence and the precautions to be used.

Suddenly X looked at his watch.

"Oh! Oh! My train leaves within forty minutes.

I've just time to go and pick up my suitcase at my hotel."

I called: "Good-bye! And good luck. . . ."

The following Friday I received a first letter from the King's Man. It is reproduced here in its exact layout to give you an idea of the language we used in our correspondence. You, who are in on it, can understand without trouble, but for the uninitiated into whose hands the letter might have fallen, the whole affair was not very clear; and though not as good as a diplomatic code, for practical purposes it was good enough for us.

29 . xii . 38

SENATE
   of
BELGIUM

My dear *Maître*:

Everything is going well, to date. Appointments are made for the second half of next week in London (N. Ch.) and in Copenhagen (the min. of the 3 Scandinavian countries). I've written to your friend in Berlin; I'll try to see him between London and Copenhagen. Tomorrow I'll have a Dutch interview here, followed perhaps by another in The Hague.

If the Copenhagen interview (the 7 and 8 of Jan.) gives good results, I shall try to follow straight through with the interviews at the two poles of the "axis", beginning with the "North Pole". . . .

As you see, it's accelerated speed, or rather flight, because it's done entirely by plane.

In case of need, I can be reached by the intermediary of M. Le Ghait, Head of the Cabinet in the Ministry of Foreign Affairs, 8 rue de la Loi, Brussels, who will be kept informed of my whereabouts. With an envelope marked *personal* and *confidential,* of course.

In a hurry, pleasant journey and a cordial greeting!

X

A second letter, which reached me just before my own departure, announced that everything was going to perfection on the British side, and with the five, and that the interview with the "friend from Berlin" had taken place, sure enough; but that some delay must be foreseen at the "North Pole", as well as the "South Pole". . . .

In Africa I was for some time without news, but that, in view of the distance separating me from the King's Man, and of my continual moving around, did not surprise me much. A short letter came, rather vague, containing, however, one point of interest which I immediately transmitted to Georges Bonnet: the King thought he could assert that Germany, given a conference, would agree that the limitation of armaments with regard to the air force should be calculated, not on the present level of our air force, but on what we should attain at some future date, to be decided upon.

Then I read in the papers that the Rome interview, Chamberlain-Halifax-Mussolini-Ciano, had led to nothing, as the King had foreseen.

When the date of January 20 approached, I scanned all the news with avidity, as you can imagine. . . . Nothing on the 20th . . . nor the 22nd, nor on the 23rd. . . . No trace of five sovereigns' letters bursting upon the sky like fireworks. "There's some hitch," I thought. As during the last days of the month I had been on a trip around the oasis of southern Tunisia, and the famous "Mareth Line," opposite the Libyan Desert, so that important news might very well have escaped my attention, on my return to Tunis I asked the Resident General, with a most innocent air:

"Since the interview in Rome has nothing notable happened on the international plane?"

"No—not a thing," he answered after a moment's cogitation.

Back in France, at the beginning of February, I got a letter from X. It was short and obscure. I understood that the King's Man, and doubtless the King himself, were trying hard not to lose confidence, but that nevertheless the magnificent hope of the outset was flying with clipped wings.

It was a month later that I saw the King's Man again. He announced his arrival in Paris by a telephone call from his hotel at the Gare de l'Est. So that he could impart his confidential information in all tranquillity of mind, I asked him to dinner at a restaurant close to the station, one well known for the convenience of its private dining-rooms and the discretion of its staff.

The King's Man was still in good spirits and had kept his will to optimism. But he had to admit failure, though with qualifications.

"Everything went admirably so long as we dealt with the Franco-British aspect, and the five in Oslo. In Berlin Abetz exerted himself. I was promised an interview with Hitler—which didn't come off. I made two trips. In Rome, in spite of the King's insistence, Mussolini managed finally not to receive me himself, turning me over to Ciano. I accepted, so as not to come home empty-handed. Ciano stood me off with fine words. I couldn't get out of him anything positive. Besides I felt clearly that, Hitler having left me in the lurch, Rome would refuse to get involved."

In the course of his eventful pilgrimage, however, and of his encounters, the King's Man had collected a mass of impressions and signs of considerable value, which he imparted to me.

"Would it be too much bother now," I asked, "if we went to talk it over with Georges Bonnet? I'm sure he'd find it of great interest."

He accepted. The meeting took place. And the conversation was indeed weighty.

As X took his leave to go back to Brussels, I felt rather gloomy. I thought: "It will have been of use in one way; it will prove on what side lies the will to understanding and peace, and on what side the opposite. . . . Neither the King nor X nor anybody else can now have the slightest doubt."

I expressed my thought aloud. X agreed, but repeated with that fine confidence of his:

"We don't admit being beaten! You yourself have said often enough that as long as nothing irreparable has occurred, one can act."

We shook hands, firmly.

Two days later it was learned that Hitler's troops were entering Prague.

"We're not pleased with Belgium," said Coulondre to me one day at the end of September 1939. (War had started on the 3rd.) "General Gamelin and Premier Daladier are much preoccupied on that account. We have a feeling that the King isn't playing square with us. And, you know, in foreign politics his role is very important."

I had him explain what caused the anxiety of Gamelin and Daladier.

"Very simple," said Coulondre. "Gamelin congratulates himself on the unexpected way in which he was able to complete his mobilization. . . . From the Maginot Line to the sea, since about the 25th, all the troops are 'buried'. They have practically nothing more to fear from air raids. . . . But suppose that in a week's time Hitler attacks through Belgium. Our contacts with the Belgian government are so unsatisfactory that we don't even know exactly what they'll do. . . . But all right, let's grant that they'll decide to defend themselves and appeal to us, by virtue of the guarantee we've given them—England and ourselves. What's terrible is that the appeal will not reach us for six hours, or perhaps twenty-four . . . and that nothing will be prepared beforehand by the staffs . . . so Gamelin will find himself called upon to send his troops forward, across the Belgian plain, under squalls of bombers, and in a general confusion inevitable with that lack of preparation. The Polish adventure gave him plenty to think about. *'Il ne s'en ressent pas'* [It sticks in his craw], as our soldiers say. . . . Worse still, we have every reason to fear, according to information received these last few days, that Hitler will have the diabolical cleverness to put through the operation in two steps: he'll attack Holland first, and he'll pretend he just wants to get to the coast, leaving Belgium aside. The Belgian government, hoping to divert the storm over their neighbour, won't budge. And having conquered Holland in the bat of an eye and established his troops along the mouths of the Scheldt, Hitler need only pick off Belgium. . . . But we ourselves shall be in an impossible position: morally obliged to march, and sure we must march in disastrous circumstances. . . . You see, General Gamelin sees it all with perfect clarity. He doesn't want another Charleroi."

"And can't we say that to the Belgians?"

Coulondre made a wry face.

"Bargeton, our Ambassador, is a very decent chap, not stupid either . . . but not very forceful—spineless. . . . On the other hand, we can't send an official note, for, understand, our strongest argument is: 'If your call comes too late and without the necessary contacts with us beforehand, it's just too bad about the guarantee—we won't march.' France can't say that in an official document, which would go through hundreds of hands, and appear in the 'yellow books.' Those things must be said looking a man squarely in the eyes. Besides, it's the King himself we must reach. . . ."

"Do you want me to try?"

"Why—certainly! If you can. . . ."

And that is why, a few days later, I left for Brussels. I had very clear instructions, but also a very great liberty of action. I could leave the Ambassador entirely out of it if I so wished. As I shared completely Gamelin's and Daladier's horror of a new Charleroi, I had made up my mind not to be content with flabby verbal assurances, with which Ambassadors are too often stuffed, and to return only after I had forced the King (and his government) to reveal his real feelings and to state where he stood.

I had informed X, in a laconic note: "I'm coming to Brussels. I count on seeing you when I get there. It's important." Since March, X had become a Minister of State. My plan was to start by disclosing the affair to him alone, then to go, with or without him, to the King.

I telephoned him on arriving. He asked me to come and get him at the Ministry, and from there he would take me home to lunch with him. "Home" was a little bachelor apartment, very bright, very modern, at the top of a new house in the suburbs of Brussels, with a magnificent view over woods (in other words, quite American). A large Flemish sergeant of a woman waited on us, and a Flemish country dish, the "carbonade", with a good Moselle wine, made the essential part of the meal.

But we talked freely only after the meal, in X's study, which was completely lined with books.

It was the first time we had seen each other since the outbreak of the present war, from which we had so ardently wished to preserve Europe.

"The fact that in the end this war took place, just the same," said I, "is frightful and humiliating for us. But now, of course, the democracies must win it, first because they did everything to avoid it—you know that better than anyone else, don't you, and the King

too?" I emphasized the allusion. ". . . Then because
they are fighting for human liberty and against the
reign of violence."

He answered less enthusiastically than I had anticipated. I told him next our anxiety in France concerning an impending attack by Hitler on the Dutch-Bel-
gian front.

He poured us a drink. I went on, laying stress on
the special danger in an attack on Holland alone.

X remained thoughtful and uncommunicative. He
asked whether I liked the drink he had poured.

"Well, have another," he said, filling my glass again.
But eventually he asked me:

"What are you going to say to the King?"

With X I could be brutal.

"Damn it all, man! I'll tell him he's got to choose.
Either he'll put us in a position to go to his help effec-
tively, or he'll face the music by himself, when the
time comes."

"What do you mean by 'put us in a position,' and
so on?"

"First, appeal to us instantly on being attacked.
. . . Next, contacts beforehand between the staffs so
that our troops need not advance blindly and at random. Last, in case Holland alone were attacked, not
to play the ostrich, but regard Belgium, *ipso facto*, as
in vital peril, and appeal to us. . . . It would in fact
be wisest to decide there is vital danger and appeal to

us as soon as the threat to Holland is unquestion-able."

X looked quite unconvinced.

"It's like this," he said: "many people here think—and I'm close to thinking so myself—that Hitler may very well be content with invading the south of Holland, and, what's more, a fairly narrow strip, without attempting anything against us afterwards. That may suffice for his strategical objectives. . . . You are asking us to court war openly."

I listened to X with stupefaction. Indeed, yes, I could guess his feelings. When a man happens to be an inveterate foe of war—the case with both of us—and to belong to a country lucky enough to be not yet at war, he won't make any move that might break that luck; he clings to the hope, however improbable, that his country will be spared the scourge, that a miracle will divert the storm. But there are limits to improbability. X was not a sentimental man. He was a logical one. How could he imagine that Hitler, once master of Holland and the mouths of the Scheldt, would resist pocketing Belgium?

He resumed:

"In any case, don't see the King first. Begin with Spaak."

"But that's contrary to our method, my dear friend."

"The King won't want to say anything without first

consulting Spaak. And Spaak would be annoyed if you passed over his head."

I went on pleading, but in vain. I was faced not exactly by a wall, but by a shock-absorbing mattress.

"A bad start," I thought, "if the King's Man is against me. . . ."

I shall give no daily detailed account here of the fight waged during the six days that followed.

I dealt chiefly with M. Spaak. I spared no effort to give him a sense of the responsibility which would weigh on him and on his sovereign.

"Suppose, within a fortnight, perhaps, Belgium finds she is invaded and we can't come to her help. In what position will you be before your conscience and in history?"

"You put me in a tragic situation!" exclaimed M. Spaak, with unfeigned emotion. "I promise you I shall explain it all to the King."

"No. I wish to say that to the King myself."

"Why? Don't you trust me to repeat your words faithfully?"

"That's not the point. If I have to go back to Paris with a negative answer, I must be able to declare positively to Premier Daladier: 'I myself said to the King all that had to be said. I'm sure he understood perfectly, and I'm sure it was with no lack of understanding, with no ambiguity, that he took the crushing responsibility of debarring his country from the help of France and England.' I have a mission. I shall carry it out. I shan't lay myself open to being told one day: 'If you had been more tenacious, if you had insisted on explaining things to the King himself, with all the force you could command, you could have averted a terrible disaster.' "

"Oh, very well," Spaak said, "I'll put it to the King. If he is willing to receive you tomorrow morning, I'll have them notify you at the hotel."

Next day Leopold III was still undecided.

"I explained the whole matter to him," said M. Spaak. "We have already deliberated on the subject —the King, the principal members of the Cabinet, and I. I swear it's very close to all our hearts."

"But why won't you let me see the King? Does he object to me personally?"

"Not in the least! What an idea! After what you did for him last winter? . . . I know about that. . . . He would receive you immediately if you were not the bearer of such a message."

"I don't understand. . . ." (In fact, I was afraid I understood too well.)

"Besides—" added M. Spaak, with painful embarrassment, "I must tell you—I don't think it's good that you should see him."

"Why?"

"How can I put it?—You may get a bad impression."

"Oh, come now!"

"You know. He's shy—silent. . . . You'll leave with a false idea perhaps . . . and pass it on over there."

"But I'm something of a psychologist. I'm able to discount an attitude that's purely on the surface. . . . Well, look here! Tell the King that I'd be willing to have him listen without having to answer a word afterwards. Let his government give me his answer. But I wish him to hear me, that's all. I'll stay in Brussels as long as need be. I'm in no hurry."

This discussion, which was often pathetic, did not prevent the advance of negotiations between M. Spaak and myself. Little by little I obtained all I had promised myself I must obtain: immediate launching of the appeal to France, without a new deliberation of the Cabinet having to take place, even if Holland alone were attacked, or only threatened in an obvious manner; contacts between the staffs through indirect ways, and so forth. And, in my mind, this was only the beginning.

On the morning of Monday the 16th—by an amusing coincidence the calendar indicated St. Leopold —M. Spaak sent for me again.

"This is what I propose to you in agreement with the King. We understand perfectly that the French government felt it could not say all this through ordinary diplomatic channels. . . . And you see we are disposed to give great weight to your arguments . . . though they go far beyond what we anticipated up to now. . . . But on your side you must understand that the King and his government are justified in making new arrangements of such consequence both for their people and for history only if they are faced with some concrete fact, which could remain just as confidential as you wish, but which will stand as a historic witness and will be our security in the future. Go back to Paris. Ask Premier Daladier for a letter in his own handwriting, which you will bring back and present to the King yourself. . . . We'll agree on the wording of the letter. Except for the King and the chief members of the Cabinet, who have taken part in our deliberations during these days, no one will hear of it. You'll return with the King's answer to the President, which must remain just as confidential. It couldn't be done, I'd say, in a more friendly, truer manner—nor one more worthy of all who took part in its negotiation."

It was then I phoned Premier Daladier, as I related in my first chapter. You know what followed.

I had told the King's Man about the principal stages of my hard task, but I felt sure that the reports I gave him were superfluous; if any man were in the know—and probably secretly consulted—he was that man!

On May 28, 1940, at eight in the morning, Paul Reynaud announced to us over the radio, in his gloomy voice, that King Leopold had capitulated in the open field. Next day we read in the papers that the Belgian government had repudiated its King and remained in France, but that the King was going to constitute in Belgium a "capitulation" government, with Henri de Man at its head.

Henri de Man—the King's Man . . . my X, my "*homme du roi*". . . .

You can realize without any trouble what my own particular reactions were. . . . For the moment, I felt my indignation was beyond all limits. To relieve my feelings I wrote a short poem in which I stigmatized the young King who had just delivered up his allies and his country. I almost wrote to Henri de Man a letter such as you can imagine. But I reflected it probably would never reach him.

All around me I could hear all kinds of very natural theories on the "betrayal" of Leopold III. He had always been secretly a Germanophil, of Fascist tendencies. The influence of his mother, Queen Elizabeth, and perhaps also the Bavarian blood of that mother, had finally conquered. From the time in 1936 when he caused the break in alliance between his country and ours, until the beginning of the war itself, he had never ceased fooling us, in connivance with Germany. At the time of the German attack he had

111

pretended to resist and appealed to the Anglo-French armies to draw them into a trap. Gamelin had vowed not to begin Charleroi over again. Thanks to his diabolical treachery, Leopold had obliged Gamelin to repeat Charleroi, and much more disastrously. Now he had put aside the mask, and with the help of a Socialist-Fascist, Henri de Man, who happened to be right at hand, he was constituting a government at Germany's beck and call.

On my own part, I could add to these conclusions of public opinion still more disturbing particulars. Henri de Man did not just happen to be there. Before this I had had occasion to smile when people in Paris or Brussels said to me: "Henri de Man has no more influence . . . the King gave him a very small position in the last Cabinet. . . ." I could reconstitute the plot much more thoroughly in depth, and farther back in time. First I could say to myself with rage: "They fooled me personally. Already in 1938 the Christmas bells masked with deceptive chiming their schemes of betrayal. . . . Who knows? Perhaps during their Berlin conversations in January 1939 Abetz and the King's Man—sham Men of Good Will —put the last touches to that part of the scenario affecting them. . . ."

I shall speak of Abetz later. Today we are concerned with the King's Man, and the King himself.

Well, now my anger has subsided, and I can live

over those events with the single passionate desire to be clear-sighted. I don't believe that the King's Man lied to me in December 1938, or that his master did. I don't believe they sought to deceive me deliberately in October 1939, or through me to deceive the French government.

True, Henri de Man had for Germany and German culture (he had been for years a professor in a Rhineland university) sympathies old and deep-rooted, which he had never hidden from me. Moreover, he had a certain mistrust of democratic methods, a belief in action, personal, direct, and even secret, and a taste for authority. He had above all a passionate love of peace and had in his heart made the same vow as mine. Circumstances led him to acquire, over a young and still pliable sovereign, an influence which could not be evaluated from the outside. He used it, in the beginning, to try certain experiments of a social order, but even more to try to preserve peace. General peace—peace for everybody—first. But when peace for everybody was smashed to bits, he hadn't the courage to admit that the peace of his own small land was nothing now but a cockleshell in a storm and that the whole problem had changed its aspect. The King and he tried to lie to themselves, until the last minute, so as not to see that the war we were fighting, in spite of ourselves, was their war. When the last minute came with its crashing eloquence, they found themselves obliged to consent to war . . . but they consented reluctantly, and lay ready for the first occasion to betray it. For when they betrayed their allies, they gave themselves the excuse that they were betraying war, primarily. . . . I shan't say their excuse was good. But when passing judgment on them, we must keep it in mind.

The tragedy of a destiny like Henri de Man's, in a way, is the tragedy, vary though it may in degree and form, of all who in Europe and throughout the world had sworn: No more war, ever! At any price!

As for King Leopold himself, the mystery that is his is linked to other enigmas. We shall come across him again.

IV

THE ENGLISH MYSTERY

WE WERE on a terrace in Portugal—one of those belvederes to be found in almost every town in that country, which commands a horizon of grace and sleeping magnificence. Around us reigned the heat, still transparent, but caressing and moist, of the end of a Portuguese spring—it was June in the year 1935. Close by, in our view, there were flowers, and scattered over the hillside there were others, unseen, the scent of which helped to make the world seem to us easygoing and mellow.

We were a few friends together there; among others, Wladimir d'Ormesson, the well-known *Figaro* critic of foreign policy, one of the few men whose opinion has always preoccupied Mussolini. "What does d'Ormesson say this morning?" was one of the questions most often put by Il Duce to his entourage, even during the present war.

We were there just casually remarking on the beauty of the scene, once again exclaiming at the charm of this country, situated at the very western limit of European soil, on whose face a perpetual musing over past splendours evokes only the smile of a sad child.

Wladimir d'Ormesson, on vacation, wasn't thinking at all of his articles for the *Figaro*. We wanted to believe that we were living in one of those times when a man had a right to be moved, privately and at leisure, without wondering at every moment whether the sky of history was not about to come crashing down over his head.

Then Antonio Ferro came up to us; Antonio Ferro was—and still is—the head of the National Propaganda of Portugal. This title, which could be disquieting, hid a deeply human man, seconded by an exquisite wife—both have lately acquired still more claim to general gratitude by the way they welcomed the refugees who came to them from France and from all the western countries submerged in the invasion.

Ferro said, with that smile of his which has never a trace of spiteful irony:

"Do you know what they tell me? England has just signed a naval pact with Hitler. It's official."

We looked at each other with dismay. Brought by

Antonio Ferro, who was at the source of information, the news couldn't be questioned. It was none the less astounding.

"Had you heard about it before leaving Paris?" I asked d'Ormesson.

"Not a word. You hadn't, either? . . . Of course, there was always something in the air about resuming the group conversations on the limitation of armaments. But this kind of thing? Not on your life! I could swear that the French government is almost as amazed as we are. It must have been warned only at the last minute, and was certainly not consulted. For it would have declared with vigour—what's just common sense—that such a pact, made behind France's back, was the best way to hinder a general settlement, as it would reassure Hitler on the British side, showing him the precarious state of Franco-British solidarity."

If we, who belonged to the people "in the know", were so greatly taken aback, then how stupefied public opinion in France must be! We could hear them say, over there, in millions of French homes: "Those Britishers, really! There's no counting on them!" And echoing, as it were, those distant murmurs, we exclaimed all together:

"Honestly, the British are incomprehensible!"

We recalled so many strange stands taken by English politics since the Treaty of Versailles. One of us quoted the curious sentence addressed by a great and clear-sighted Englishman, at the beginning of the eighteenth century, to his compatriots, reproaching them for their conduct towards Holland, after the wars fought together against Louis XIV:

"You hide from your allies and take counsel with your enemies; you discourage the former in their insistence; you encourage the latter in their resistance." Wasn't that the whole story of the relations between England, France, and Germany from 1919 on?

But what was an aggravating game between 1919 and 1930 turned in 1935 into a challenge to fate. The German peril had never ceased to grow. Since the coming of the Nazi regime it had been taking a concrete and obsessing form. True, there were many ways of envisaging the struggle against that peril. I was one of those—and d'Ormesson, too, I think—to whom recourse to force or any manner of "preventive warfare" was repugnant. Since we had been stupid enough not to prevent Hitler's rise to power when it was relatively easy, we weren't going to jump on him now that he had succeeded in getting the German people behind him. We were too strongly persuaded that nothing good can ever come from war in general. Besides, there still rang in our ears the indignant clamour with which Europe and America, twelve years earlier, had greeted our occupation of the Ruhr. . . . (I rather hope that those who in 1923 raised all that indignant clamour are feeling a little silly in 1940. They have their own small part in the psychological responsibility for the "collapse" of the democracies.)

So in 1935, resort to force being out of the question, it seemed to us we could still hope, by shrewd politics, to weaken the internal and external virulence of Nazism and to prepare the time when the plague could be wiped out in less gory ways, taking advantage of an opportunity which could not fail to turn up sooner or later. It was a point of view shared by a number of Englishmen, one I had often heard stated in their country. But how could they not see that the only chance of stemming the German peril in such a manner was a community of thought and action, indissoluble and above suspicion, between France and England?

On the Portuguese terrace we spoke of the "English mystery". Each one of us had anecdotes to tell, characteristic traits to cite.

And today, here in New York, in the ending of the tragic summer of 1940, I find the English mystery once again in the path of my meditations.

Yet I almost ruled it out of this book for two reasons. First, at a time when England, left standing alone, is fighting magnificently for the freedoms and honour of the world, I should not wish to say a single word which might cast doubt upon the admiration and affection I feel for her, or which might diminish

119

in the slightest the wave of active sympathy which is carrying this continent towards her. But I have spoken, and shall continue to speak, with entire frankness about the errors of my country. I have no right to conceal the errors of England in the recent past, or her faults in evaluation. That would distort the picture too much. Besides, they weigh too heavily on our shoulders, and on hers. They may make a good subject for meditation for nations still able to ask themselves what their own conduct shall be.

My second reason for hesitating was the fear of disappointing my readers. This time I cannot offer sketches as specific and dramatic as in other connections. And since I allow myself neither to invent the slightest thing nor to add romantic detail to the stark truth, there's a chance they'll find my "English mystery" drab and blurred. And yet there is no country I have visited more often than England, nor is there any question which has seemed to me more worthy of incessant effort than that of Anglo-French relations.

As I think it over, I believe it is the nature of the present "English mystery" to be drab and blurred . . . and, further, to remain anonymous. You see, what came off my pen was not "the mystery of Chamberlain", nor "the mystery of Baldwin", nor anything else of that kind. At a pinch, it probably wouldn't be impossible to write "mystery of Edward VIII". But if we had to stay on the level of high politics, the chapter would be slim and reduced to a few brief episodes, themselves shrouded in obscurity. . . . We'll touch upon it when we put the question: "Who saved Fascism?"

Yes, the English mystery, during these last twenty years, is by its very nature a collective and diffuse mystery. But that doesn't lessen its interest—quite the contrary—nor does it exempt us from looking into it.

Besides, whenever I've had the opportunity of asking French or European leaders about their English experiences, they've all said: "Yes, quite true; we've never had the impression of dealing with some special person." In other words, with a man whose individual character, disposition, and will must be taken specifically into account in making one's calculations. "We had to do with England, contradictory and internally complicated as she is . . . with the layers of English opinion and society . . . with institutions, public or private, official or occult, for which one man or other happened momentarily to be the spokesman."

There's an element of historical chance here, certainly. The outstanding personalities that put their stamp on other periods of English history are not to be found in this one. They must have sought an outlet in other directions. Where, in the political world of contemporary Great Britain, can we find an equivalent for the great figures so numerous in literature and science? . . . Or else, if a strong and luminous personality did try to clear a path for himself through politics, sooner or later he stumbled into obstacles and was forced to give way to more authentic—more interchangeable—representatives of "general and diffuse" England. That's what happened to Mr. Eden. I have always been surprised that a mind of the highest calibre, like Harold Nicolson's, so fitted to understand things French, was not put to better use in the highest posts. Even Mr. Winston Churchill had to wait till the War of France was lost before being admitted to command. There is no doubt that the aversion in British politics to great figures has been very costly to both England and France, and therefore to the whole world.

I remember that once I had the impression of being suddenly faced by the "English mystery," and experienced an intellectual discomfort that I still feel. It was in 1931, during a journey through the Orient and Asia Minor.

I had stayed in Egypt first, and spent a fairly long time with the French directors of the Suez Canal. They showed me on the spot how the thing worked. They spoke to me about the English, joked pleasantly about them.

"Do you mean to tell me," I exclaimed, "that with

the proportion of capital they hold in the company, and, above all, the political control they exercise over Egypt, the British have left all the technical direction of the canal in French hands, from the very start? You find that natural, because you are used to it. But consider what the canal represents to a nation which places the mastery of maritime routes above everything else. After all, you were free to sabotage it when you wished?"

"Absolutely. . . . They trust us."

"Today we are friends of England; but we weren't always. You must admit that it's prodigious."

They agreed. We joined in admiration of the "gentlemanly" aspect of such a procedure, and of the unexampled liberalism it presupposed on the part of England. "Show me another country," said I, "which possessing such supremacy—and so many ways of being a nuisance—would have used it with such moderation . . . to the extent that one ends by not even noticing it, as in your case . . . and by not thinking about it."

I arrived in Asia Minor still steeped in this impression of chivalry, and pondering over it. Already at Jerusalem, when I asked the French consul about his relations with the British, who had the mandate over Palestine, he answered to my great surprise that things weren't very cordial, nor very above-board, though he personally hadn't much to complain of. "But you'll see in Syria. Try to make our officers talk."

In Syria it was France that held the mandate. We had had terrible difficulties, of which the country still bore marks, and anxiety had by no means died out. As I drove through the country, they kept telling me: "See that hollow over there, that's one of the places the gangs of Druses came through . . ." or: "These gardens that we're crossing, it used to be impossible to have troops march through. Shots were fired from each clump of trees. . . ." Before long the officers said to me: "Behind it all are the British."

"What a tale to tell me! That's absurd!"

They gave me precise facts, proofs. . . . They had a service of information whose job was precisely to clear up such problems. Besides, the officers were young men and gay. They couldn't be suspected of giving in to a persecution complex. But still I argued:

"Come now! You can't make me believe that England is wasting her time, arming tribes of plunderers against us, and subsidizing agents to keep local agitations alive! England isn't crazy. She knows perfectly well that our interests in Asia Minor are hers, that it's not we that she need fear, and that our troops here contribute to the security of her Empire."

The young officers answered with a smile:

"You don't know the Intelligence Service!"

In a journey to London, a very few weeks after my

return, I put the question openly to my English friends, high in office. They were almost as troubled as I was. They said:

"The British government is certainly not involved in all those intrigues. It is even probable that it knows nothing about them." They explained to me: "You know we're a peculiar country. . . . Great Britain is a bundle of institutions, each one having its own traditions, often very old, and a certain jealous autonomy. Each one is convinced that it's perfectly able, without interference, to see its duty and to work its hardest to uphold the greatness of the Empire."

One of them observed, humorously:

"Perhaps the Intelligence Service, at least in the Near East, hasn't noticed that something has changed between you and us since the time of Fashoda. . . ." He went on: "But the position of the Intelligence Service is by no means unique. . . . Keep in mind that the High Church, the big universities, the City of London, the aristocracy, the nonconformist churches, and heaven knows what else, are so many moral and material forces, each with its own driving impulse. The impulses may happen to coincide. But it's by chance."

In all truth, I must remark that not one of my interlocutors thought of formulating the following conclusion:

"As such a state of things is the cause of shocking

discrepancies and serious weaknesses in our national action, we must modify it as quickly as possible."

Everyone seemed to regard these institutions as forces of nature. You have the right to be sorry that the London climate is cold and rainy. But what can you do about it? And, after all, who knows? It may have its points. At the back of his mind, each of the men I talked to certainly had the idea that such a state of affairs must have its points. . . . Alas, we had just come upon days when other nations were tightening up in a fiercely "totalitarian" spirit and pitilessly doing away with their internal differences, soon to throw themselves into the struggle with all their energies, head on.

In Paris, at the time, when I talked with my political friends—Painlevé, Herriot, and others—about the English attitude towards us, they expressed the same anxiety: "England is not satisfied with us. She doesn't back us. She evidently disapproves of our politics. . . . But she doesn't indicate very clearly what political line she'd like us to take."

As most of them were then in the opposition, they were inclined to think that England was right, and that if English opinions didn't seem clear to us, it was because our government did all it could to cloud them.

But when, after the 1932 elections, they came back into power—they or their friends—they had to acknowledge that only one thing was clear: English dissatisfaction with us; and apart from that, when it came to knowing what the English expected of us and proposed to do on their side, it was black as ink.

In the autumn following the 1932 elections, I took upon myself a quite unofficial mission to London. I did not go to question men in the English government, since, after all, my political friends in France had innumerable opportunities and every facility for that themselves, and since it was from just such conversations that they failed to draw anything precise. I went, rather, to try to reach that elusive thing, English thought, by a detour, talking with important people who had no official capacity and would therefore be less handicapped in the feat so difficult for any Englishman: to get it off his chest. I had talks of considerable interest, which have rendered me valuable service ever since whenever I have been faced with a problem in the psychology of the British nation. They were real "revelations", one might say, but of a human order; and when I had to translate them into practical terms for my political friends in France, the results seemed disappointing.

"In the first place," I came back saying, "the English spent more than a year before the elections being very mad at France. We suspected it, but not to such an extent. If we had suddenly been faced with a difficult situation, we'd probably have had them against us. I don't know if our government realized it at the time. But the people knew nothing about it; and had that day come, they'd have been astounded. . . . That explains, too, why things went so badly on the German side. . . . Well, that's ancient history. . . ."

We'll note, parenthetically, that it was ancient history by the autumn of 1932, perhaps, but that just the same it was very unfortunate history, as it corresponded neatly, alas, with the period when, in Germany, Hitler was playing the hardest game of his match. In 1931 Hitler was nothing in Germany's sky but a big storm-cloud, which it was up to us to disperse. But entirely aside from more positive and semi-official complicity on the part of England (and there was some, without doubt, alas!), official England gave support to Hitler in Germany every time she pretended to drift away from us. . . . In the autumn of 1932 Hitler was solidly entrenched. But let's get on.

"In the second place," I went on, "as to our future relations. I said to the English: 'Now you are going to deal with Leftist governments, with Ministers of Foreign Affairs named Herriot, Daladier, Paul-Boncour. . . . I give my word they regard you with the greatest good will. Suppose one of them were here and asked: "What must I do so that past mistakes won't be repeated? What line must I take to be in real agreement with England? Tell me frankly, man to man." ' They answered: 'Well, we'd say to them:

128

"Just go right through all these conservatives, these lords and such. . . . Appeal to the *English conscience*."' I pointed out that as practical advice to be transmitted to a Minister of Foreign Affairs, that was rather vague. They replied: 'Well, put it this way: when you need to have our people solidly with you, don't be satisfied to exchange notes with the London government. Prove to the moral élite of England the validity of your cause, by real arguments; the élite will side with you, and you'll see, the government will have to follow.'"

It won't surprise you to hear that my political friends made rather wry faces. They certainly were not men to disregard moral forces, any more than I. But this England, asking us to appeal to her "conscience" when grave and urgent decisions had to be taken, promised many an uncomfortable minute for our government!

You know how it is with couples, often happily married—before an evening out, or a week-end, the husband anxiously asks his wife: "Where should you like to go?" His wife answers: "Oh, I don't know. I haven't the faintest idea. . . ." The husband insists. "You know what I like," says the wife, "you choose. . . ." Then the husband wears himself out with suggestions, each met with a discouraging little pout. In despair, he finally chooses. But, alas, he knows beforehand that in the middle of the evening or the walk his wife will heave a sigh and exclaim: "What ever gave you the idea of coming here! You might have guessed it wasn't what I felt like."

To question the *English conscience* every time the decisive hour struck was about as risky a business as for the husband to guess what his wife "really felt like."

Failing anything better, we came, all of us, to the following practical conclusion: "Since there's no pleasing the English, and since they refuse to declare beforehand what they want, we'll say to them: 'We probably don't know how to go about it, particularly with Germany. You know her and feel her out probably better than we do. So take charge of her, at least for a while. What you do will be well done. At least, that way, we hope we'll be spared further reproaches.'"

I myself wrote an article to that effect. One day Painlevé said to me (it was a very few months before his premature death. He had twice just missed being President of the Republic. Even when he was not in power, he exercised great influence on the Leftist governments, by his intellectual prestige): "Yes, you're right. We'll let the English carry their responsibilities for a bit. They'll see how pleasant it is to argue with Germany."

I'm sorry now that I had my share in recommending that attitude. It would have been excellent had the aim been to give England a chance to learn and to reflect. But it was no longer a time for schooling. We were going to let Nazi Germany seize advantages never to be recaptured. And the time England lost thinking over her disappointing experiences, she could not use for arming.

Yet it is true that they had not fed me empty phrases in London in 1932, and the "English conscience" was not a myth. The proof would come three years later, in 1935. Then it did decide to speak—to speak very loudly, in a voice that suddenly thrilled the world.

But, alas, deplorable changes had come about in France. There were no more Leftist governments—through their own fault. The collapse of the Daladier of February 6 and 7, 1934 opened the way to a series of reactionary governments, limited in their realism, who shrugged their shoulders when moral ideas were invoked, and in whose ears the voice of the "English conscience" spoke words either meaningless or open to suspicion of hypocrisy.

It was a tragic situation for the world, which has not yet quite grasped it. Historians in the future will ponder over this strange combination of events, in which the whole destiny of the twentieth century just missed taking another direction. I shall devote a whole chapter, the last of the seven, to this event, which I followed closely. The subject is worth it, both for its extreme importance and for the mystery which still shrouds it. The outline is familiar to the public, but the underlying circumstances are unknown, except to a few initiates; of that I am sure every time I talk about it to people, even in well-informed circles.

It concerns what was called, very humbly, the Ethiopian question. (History will find a name more worthy of what was at stake.) As I shall come back to it later, I'll give only indispensable facts here. You recall that in 1935, Mussolini having prepared more and more obviously and heavily for a move against Ethiopia, which was a member of the League of Nations, the English government began to show belated signs of anxiety, made increasingly insistent representations to Italy, along with proposals of its good offices and those of the French government, grudgingly granted. Up to that time it was a diplomatic affair, just more troublesome than most. But it was about to become a great human affair. Its development in the chancelleries coincided with a vast movement of the English conscience, in favour of the organization of peace and a decisive reinforcement of the League of Nations: the Peace Ballot. This movement, quite spontaneous and springing from most noble motives, encountered the Ethiopian question, which became for the awakened British conscience a highly significant case, a decisive test. If Ethiopia, a member of the League of Nations, was abandoned to Italian greed, then there must be no more talk of the League of Nations or of international justice. All the work of the last sixteen years in that direction was nothing but a sinister joke. But if the League, referred to in due form, obliged the aggressor to withdraw at the last moment, or condemned the aggression to failure if it was attempted, then proof would be given that even in the most acute of crises justice could win over violence. All of humanity's hopes for the future could flourish.

You know roughly what happened: the League charged itself with the affair. It gave Italy a solemn warning. Mussolini disregarded it. The League voted sanctions which were to be applied by all League members, providing for progressive severity if the country guilty of rebellion against the law of nations held them in contempt. England—not yet officially, indeed—offered her fleet, should anything further be necessary. Covertly encouraged by the French government of the moment, Mussolini persisted, invaded Ethiopia, terrorized the poor army of the Negus by using massed aviation, thus for the first time applying a method destined for wide use in other theatres of war. Disconcerted, the League members applied sanctions more and more halfheartedly. England herself, little by little, gave in.

133

By the beginning of 1936 Mussolini had finished the business; Ethiopia was practically conquered, the League taxed with helplessness; the defenders of peace and international justice everywhere were discouraged and appalled about what was to follow.

What did follow was the entrance of Hitler's troops into the Rhineland, then the Spanish war, then Japanese aggression against China, then the Anschluss with Austria, and so on. The floodgates of war were opened on the world. The flood is not yet at an end.

By the end of 1935 the Leftist parties in France, who were then in the opposition, saw very clearly the mistake made by the Laval government, and the consequent criminal attack on the future of peace. Moreover, they knew that the days of the government were numbered, and that before long they themselves would take over once more the responsibilities of power and of our foreign policy, even before the elections of 1936. So they were anxious to understand as nearly as they could how the Ethiopian affair had developed.

One day in mid-November I had a long talk with Maurice Sarraut. Maurice Sarraut (the brother of Albert), manager of the *Dépêche de Toulouse*, has been one of the purest, most modest, and at the same time most influential figures in the Third Republic. When offered the highest offices, he has refused, as I can bear witness. But no grave decision was made in the republican party (in the broad sense of the word "republican"), no cabinet was formed, without consulting him in some way or other. Even the Rightists respected him. It's no exaggeration to say that he has been for years a kind of President of the Republic behind the scenes.

"I know," Maurice Sarraut said, "that you're going to England. One question is on my mind. You'd do us a good turn by trying to throw light on it. . . . Mussolini's preparations against Ethiopia started almost the first of the year. Already in March, in April, they hit you in the eye. England appeared to notice nothing. She couldn't be blind to a situation the entire press was discussing. But it was not till May that she showed signs of anxiety. That's what seems strange to us . . . and what must be cleared up for our future conduct."

"Quite. . . . But you're getting at something further?"

"I can't help wondering if England didn't do it on purpose. Yes. . . . Maybe she gave him enough rope to hang himself, to be sure of having him there to finish off when she pleased. Mind you, I'd call that fighting fair. . . . But according as that hypothesis is true or false, England's present set-up must be interpreted differently, and we must anticipate quite different reactions from her in the future."

It was certainly a most interesting problem. In

London I started working on it. From the English I got very little, as was to be expected. Only two or three ranking members of the government could have answered me with certainty. You can't imagine them saying to me: "But of course, my dear sir, we let Mussolini walk right into the trap. . . . We're delighted with the result." But in London there was one man who had been in unbroken contact with the British government, who, piecing together the slight indications gleaned from day to day, helped by his thorough knowledge of the British soul, could form an opinion: our Ambassador, M. Corbin. I felt sure that the French government itself had never put the question to him. It's hard to believe what reticence is exercised in such respects between a government and its ambassador. Inquisitiveness would seem a lack of *savoir-vivre*, especially when dealing with a friendly country. If need be, one makes some allusions in a conversation that leaves no traces; never in a dispatch.

I told M. Corbin frankly that my intention was to sound him out in the name of the French government "of tomorrow"; in no sense to act badly by the present government, however questionable its politics seemed to us, but out of solicitude for the permanent interests of France. M. Corbin, who is a republican and a patriot, understood perfectly. He pondered, sought for the right words:

"Taking everything into account, my answer is: No,

I don't think there was any kind of premeditation on the part of the English. . . . I watched them closely through all that time. . . . I think I know them fairly well. . . . You see, this has to do with mysteries of English politics which make so many people misjudge her. . . . For instance, they say the English are per-fidious . . . they like long-drawn out machinations. That's not true. In fact, the English never foresee any-thing. That can be very serious in some cases. . . . They rely on their instinct. But their instinct, though often clear-sighted, is also short-sighted. . . . They not only don't try to see ahead, but when it's some-thing bothersome, the later they see, the better. Mus-solini's massing of troops in Africa can't have escaped them. But as long as they could, they said to them-selves: 'We mustn't exaggerate . . . we mustn't make the thing worse by shouting too soon. . . . Things may shake down without any fuss. . . .' The English always think things will shake down. . . . Then they obviously tried to make the best use, or the least bad, of a situation they neither wanted nor foresaw. They improvised counterthrusts or parries—some rather un-fortunate, like the naval pact with Hitler. . . . Even now I'm certain they don't know where they're headed. Now that Mussolini is in the trap—which he set for himself—will they make the most of that to finish up with him and Fascism both? I don't know. But certainly they themselves don't."

Nothing I had been told since I heard Great Britain called a "bundle of autonomous and jealous institutions" helped me more to take for granted the peculiarities of British politics.

During the second half of 1936 and all through 1937 we were very much preoccupied in Paris with the Spanish war, its possible developments, and the riddles it offered. I often saw the Minister of Foreign Affairs, my friend Delbos, and in all our conversations I had a slight feeling of personal responsibility, since without me, as I related in my first chapter, Delbos would probably not have held that office. My guiding thought—and it was Delbos's too—continued to be: "Always, everywhere, we must work to lessen the risk of war. The totalitarian powers are apparently trying to use Spain to start a fight, and in any case to sap our strength. Let's not fall into their trap, letting ourselves be drawn step by step from limited intervention to a general war, which we would enter under most unfortunate material and moral conditions. But, just the same, don't let's allow our enemies to gain decisive advantages over there, which would only make war certain in the years to come, and condemn us beforehand to lose it." Needless to say, the game Russia was playing seemed to us most ambiguous, and part of our work lay in keeping the Popular Front government from blind acceptance of Communist catchwords. But the English game didn't always seem exactly clear to us either. "Would they like a victory for the Spanish Republicans? Or for Franco?" Delbos would say. "I can never find out."

In November 1937 I was staying in London. It gave me a new and remarkable opportunity to sense British complexity. The first people I met belonged to intellectual circles. They flaunted an unalloyed sympathy for the Spanish Republicans, unhampered by any consideration of political expediency. An observer unaccustomed to English contradictions would have thought: "We're in a country governed democratically, by public opinion, and the government must think along the same lines as these people, but with more reserves."

At the French Embassy, as M. Corbin happened to be away, I talked with his chief associates, and with one in particular. I was much struck by what was said to me, with an enigmatic air of satisfaction: "They needn't worry too much in Paris. The English government doesn't look disapprovingly at the headway Franco is making. It has its good reasons for that." "But that's very serious," I replied, "it's just those reasons we need to know. Have they secured formal assurances and guarantees from Franco? We don't intend to be taken in by the more or less blind inclinations of English conservatives. They can't get out of it by saying with a wink: 'Don't worry!' The

French government will make its own evaluations. For instance, Franco's promise that he would see to the interests of the Rio Tinto stockholders would be judged quite inadequate."

Two days later I had a conversation more disturbing still. A person of consequence in England—who wouldn't allow his name to be used—declared: "Warn your government. Desperately serious things are happening. Our conservatives are idiots and criminals. . . . I can assure you that at this very moment, in November 1937, the City of London—oh, not the whole city, but powerful elements in it—is still advancing heavy loans to Hitler for his intensive armament; in fact, is subsidizing his rearmament, which without them would be about to snuff out."

"But that's impossible!" I exclaimed. "They're not traitors!"

"No, they're rather stupid people, who see above all a good opportunity for investment. . . . A City financier can't resist the temptation of an investment, even with the murderer of his own father. Besides, don't forget that those people have a terror of bolshevism that condemns them to blindness in other directions. . . . Naturally, they hope Franco will win. . . . I wouldn't say they hope Hitler will, but it's certain they don't want him to lose. . . . Anyway, you know perfectly well that its roots go far back, and without those people Hitler would never have come to power. . . . A part of the high aristocracy, too, has always worked in the same direction."

I was deeply troubled by such assertions, the sincerity of which I could not question. I mentioned the subject first to Harold Nicolson, at the end of a luncheon in my honour, over which he had been kind enough to preside. He was reassuring, on the whole: "I don't think there can be a heavy financing of Hitler. The government would know and wouldn't allow it. But it's unfortunately not out of the question that capital, in free circulation on the market, might in the end be used, more or less indirectly, for Hitler's benefit. . . . Anyway, you were right to tell me about it. We can't be too much on our guard."

I went back to the French Embassy and said something like this: "I have no way to check what this information is worth. I don't know whether you have. But, given its source, we have no right to pass it by. The English government is certainly acting in good faith. We must put the thing before them. Paris can't do it—not at this point—without proofs. But in the course of friendly conversations, you can always slip in a casual: 'That's what we've been told. . . . Is there any truth in it?'"

Another eminent personality, foreign, but well informed, opened further perspectives: "You appear to be suffering in Paris because you don't see sufficiently clearly into the intentions of your English friends.

. . . More specifically, you're wondering when they'll make up their minds that the German peril is of the first magnitude and that everything must be done to ward it off. . . . Well now, I'll give you my impression. It's not a certainty—but it fits many indications. The English government dreams along, more or less like this—for it has no real plan; I believe as you do that the English don't make any plans, but they scent out the future in one way or another, and eventually their behaviour is affected by it. Well, the English government, and most of the conservatives, think that probably there's no way of preventing war in so sick a Europe . . . and the wise thing would be to divert it from the West. . . . They can easily picture a Germany throwing itself on Russia . . . to do that, she'd have to knock Poland about a little, but that's a detail. With Hitler busy in Russia, there'd be a breathing-space . . . he might break his own neck there! Anyway, Germany would come back sobered for a while. . . . Of course, the Soviets must have no chance of winning; that would be the end of everything."

"And that explains the alleged leaning of British finance towards Hitler."

"Exactly. . . . Their dream—for I insist it's only a dream—would be to make one evil destroy the other, while the West looked on, in the best possible position, and then helped restore order."

142

"Yes," thought I, "it's pretty cynical—though not more so than its perfect counterpart, dreamed by Stalin at this moment—but it isn't so stupid, after all, and so far as subtlety is concerned, English conservatives may actually be worth more than they're reputed to be. . . . If that's their dream, then they'd do better to talk it over openly with their French friends instead of leaving us in such doubt. . . . It's true I can't picture a Popular Front government called upon to deliberate on that kind of program!"

Don't think, however, that it was the existence in Paris of an already much subdued Popular Front government which kept the English from being more definite. The indecisions and contradictions were rooted in themselves.

I have seen all our Ministers of Foreign Affairs fall prey to the same insecurity of thought, not touching the friendliness of England, which they had judged to be sure and solid, but touching the intentions, inclinations, and dreams of British politics and the extraordinary difficulty of prevailing upon the English to take a stand. I can still hear Paul-Boncour exclaiming in my presence, in the short period of 1938 when he was Minister: "Ha! Did you see that? I gave the English a jolt! I managed to pull something fairly definite out of them! . . . You've got to speak sternly to them!" He was alluding to the speech Mr.

143

Neville Chamberlain had just made, in which he let it be understood that England did not consider herself entirely unconcerned in the eventual fate of Czechoslovakia. Paul-Boncour attributed this spurt of "definiteness" to his intervention, and there's no doubt he was right in thinking that the English must be spoken to sternly. But he forgot to state what had just taken place to give England a jolt: the Anschluss. If the English had to be presented with an Anschluss every six months to keep them in good moral health, there was no telling where that would take us.

And it certainly took us far.

I could give other instances when, as witness or confidant, I saw the real fits of anguish into which the "English mystery" sometimes plunged our leaders during the years just before the war. But I think I can sum up the matter more clearly in a short symbolical scene. Visualize the office at the Quai d'Orsay, of which I spoke earlier. Imagine the French Minister of Foreign Affairs—be his name Delbos, Paul-Boncour, or Georges Bonnet—between two telephone calls to London, pacing dejectedly round this office, soliloquizing thus:

"The English are pretty decent. . . . In fact, they're our only reliable friends in Europe. . . . The others, well—there are, in the East, well-meaning nations who'd have a liking for us, but they're in the hands of adventurers and swindlers. . . . Childish to count on them. But the English—well, they're solid and they're gentlemen. . . . We're with them, first and always! No question about that. . . . But they're an awful nuisance. . . . They're always afraid they'll get involved, or make a step too soon. . . . They say they don't want to get tied up any further on the Continent. What does that mean? . . . The Continent won't ask what they think. They know they can't escape a war let loose on the Continent, in which we'd be caught ourselves. So can't they see that the only way to prevent it is to state openly that they're in it single-heartedly, and to prepare single-heartedly? . . . What are they afraid of? That we'll rush around smashing things and getting into war without having to? Granted they could think such nonsense in 1923 . . . but now! They aren't so stupid as that! . . . Well? . . . There are people who say to us: 'The English are humouring Hitler a little. They think they need him as a rampart against bolshevism. They'll let you try to keep him in his place, but they won't do anything which might bring about his fall. It's even said that they allow capital and raw materials to slip by into Göring's armament factories. . . .' Hard to question them bluntly on the subject. These aren't questions one asks a friend. . . . No, they're not double-dealers. They've a mania for precaution and procrastination. They're always afraid that by taking their stand squarely, they'll ruin their chance for some feasible arrangement. . . . To be wise, in their eyes, is to maintain, as long as possible, the chance for any feasible arrangement. That's very fine. But contradictory arrangements do exist, so they condemn themselves to live in the midst of contradiction."

When like soliloquies took place in 1938, there would be inserted:

"What an idea, sending Lord Runciman to Czechoslovakia to investigate!—the same old fondness for dragging things out ambiguously, for nursing along all possibilities for compromise. . . . They hope to intimidate Beneš, and to make us more manageable. . . . But don't they see that it's Berlin they'll make more unmanageable, by letting it think that London fundamentally disapproves of us and will drop us at the last minute?"

In 1939 little change was needed to bring the soliloquy up to date: replace Czechoslovakia by Poland. . . . At just such times I heard Georges Bonnet say, with a shrug of his tired shoulders: "The English are terrible."

After the war was on, the soliloquy was often transferred to the office in the rue Saint-Dominique. The procrastinations and indecisions of England had shifted in orientation but not in nature. They now bore upon the conduct of the war. It's still too soon to write their story. But when diplomatic initiative

146

was needed, or daring in military ventures, I felt all too often that the instinctive hesitations of our government were increased or excused by England's hesitations; in fact, merely by the fear of her hesitation. How many times I have heard, when an excuse for lack of audacity was sought: "Anyway, the English wouldn't have it." Certainly neither Gamelin nor Daladier nor others needed this perpetual jamming on of brakes.

The conclusion isn't hard to draw. It's plain to read in these pages. England has been victim first of her famous "Wait and see," which under analysis, as someone said, falls into two formulas: "Wait and don't see, wait and don't act." She suffered from the autonomy, the selfishness even, of her institutions, her large organizations and social forces, each of which followed its respective traditions or particular impulses and had its own ideas about the hierarchy of perils. . . . Some of these evils are common to all free nations and are the price of their liberty. But with the English the disadvantages inherent in a regime of democratic discussion—disadvantages which men must accept if they wish to remain free, reducing them as best they can—happened to reinforce a profound trait of national psychology, to the extent that it justified the biting comment: "The English invented parliamentary government to give their

147

natural hesitations the majesty of law." Quite possibly it was not a very good chance, during such decisive years, that the conservatives were in power—the most timorous of them, at that. They'd have rendered better service at a different time. More than anybody else, they were inclined to exaggerate the bolshevist peril, to delude themselves about the situation in Spain or the "good points" of Mussolini and Hitler, to close their eyes, perhaps, to the serious conniving of which the business world and the aristocracy were guilty, to dream of diversions in the East, which were senseless unless the West had decided to use in politics a Machiavellian boldness, repugnant to all the moral forces which it contained and championed.

But perhaps the greatest error of England (and of France, too) was that she was not sure enough of her mission, of the inalienable sanctity of the cause she represented; she did not listen with sufficient reverence to the dictates of that "English conscience" they told me about in 1932. When she listened to them in 1935, she was very close to saving the world. I think she is listening to them now. May it not be too late for her to save the world this time!

V

THE NAZI MYSTERY

I was on the Hamburg-Berlin express one late afternoon in November 1934. It was already dark. I could
see the first lights of the suburbs. There was neither
rain nor mist.

I was quite deeply moved. It was my first real visit
since the Nazis had taken possession of Germany, to
which I had come so often at the time of the Weimar
Republic. I had passed through it rapidly only twice;
in the autumn of 1933, returning from Denmark, and
in the month of May of that very year 1934, on my
way to Rumania, via Poland and Bukovina. On both
occasions I had stayed in Berlin barely a day, just long
enough to catch a glimpse, on Unter den Linden, of
small processions of men in uniform under swastika
flags, and to note the fact that in other respects life
in the capital hadn't undergone startling changes. I'd

made no personal contacts, except, in May, with the French Ambassador. Actually I still had everything to discover about the monstrous phenomenon which the world was discussing with increasing preoccupation. I thought I knew earlier Germany fairly well; between 1920 and 1930 I had formed numerous friendships there. But the better I thought I knew her, the more anxious I was to know what she could have become in the hands of those Nazi leaders, most of whose names were unknown yesterday, and who came from levels of society into which my explorations had never taken me. I had, besides, as you will see, other reasons more pressing than pure curiosity. The Franco-German problem seemed to me to have reached a dangerously novel phase. Whatever course of action was to be taken, I felt that the time for shilly-shallying was past, and that we could afford no more errors.

On the station platform I saw a group coming towards me. It was made up of two or three "civilians", and three or four young men wearing uniforms which looked to me like storm-troopers'. One of the two civilians, whom I'll call A, for the time being, was a young man, well set up and pleasant, whose acquaintance I had made a few weeks before, in Paris. The young men in uniform seized my suitcases; A inquired warmly about my journey; and we went out. Two open cars were waiting for us, carrying the swastika pennant. The car piloting us went off at high speed. I was in the second, with A at my left. The young Nazi who seemed to be the leader of his comrades in uniform, whom I'll call Hermann—I've forgotten his real name—sat opposite me, on the folding seat. He said to me, in rather slow but correct French:

"We were told the hour of your arrival a little too late. Otherwise we'd have received you more fittingly."

I couldn't imagine what more he wanted. As for me, I found our little procession quite pompous enough as it was. As we passed, the "schupos", standing stiffly in the evening light, saluted us. The people in the street glanced our way.

The trip from the station to the Hotel Adlon, where they were putting me up, was quickly made. The manager was there to greet me; the staff showered attentions on me. Clearly nothing had been left to chance.

The aim, the pretext rather, of my journey was a lecture I had been asked to give. I knew it would take place in one of the University halls, before a selected audience, which would include young men (students, I thought). I had no other details.

A few minutes before the lecture, which was at eight in the evening, two cars came for me, as they had at the station. But this time the one intended for me was a closed car. To go towards the University we had only to follow straight along Unter den Linden. I settled back into my corner, thinking over what I was going to say, and wondering what my contact would be with an audience so different from the ones I had known here in Berlin itself. I hardly glanced out. Besides, the large square to which we were coming, at the end of Unter den Linden, was badly lighted at night. Our two cars drove around it, so as to draw up with the north pavement on their right.

As I got out of my car, the first thing I saw, under the street lamps, was the stretch of empty pavement —which is very wide at that place—between two rows of men in uniform, who were holding back a small crowd of onlookers on both sides. An order rang out. The two rows stood at attention and saluted with raised arm. I walked forward, rather dumbfounded, towards a wide open iron gate, accompanied by my escort, who, having shown me the way, contrived to fall back two steps. What could I do but keep on walking, looking like someone who took it all for granted? I reached the gate. At the back of a courtyard a flight of steps and a portico led up to a building. Two rows of uniforms stretched the full length of the courtyard, on one side men dressed more or less like infantry (but who, perhaps, were not infantry); on the other, men dressed like sailors (but who maybe weren't sailors, either). They carried no arms; but some at least carried accessories I had no time to examine. The two ranks were at salute. But all that was nothing. As I passed through the gateway, a Wagnerian fanfare burst over our heads; it came from a score of strapping fellows, in uniform like the rest, stationed on a balcony which looked over the flight of steps at the entrance; their long horns, like those of the heralds-at-arms in the *Ring*, spread like a great fan. The display went on inside the building. I crossed a hall and went up to a staircase between two rows of young guards, standing on each step. And that is how I was "canalized" to a rostrum, the entrance to which I found with some difficulty, as it had been turned into a mountain of flowers—chrysanthemums of all shades, if I remember rightly. It was from the very bosom of that mountain of flowers, out of which I emerged only from the chest up, that I was going to speak. Ample folds of bunting in the French colours draped the walls of the room.

I couldn't fail to find such a setting most extraordinary. But I did not lose my presence of mind. As I began to deliver the first sentences in French, I studied the audience in front of me, which was really new in my experience. The first rows were occupied by some men in brown shirts, who, judging from the brilliance of their insignia, must have been high dignitaries in the party, and by some hundred civilians, among whom I recognized scarcely a face except that of the French Ambassador, my friend François-Poncet, and that of the translator of my plays, a Jew. All the rest was made up of "brown shirts", decorated with special insignia that meant nothing to me, almost all young men. Were they, then, the "students"? I soon realized I needn't worry about a cold audience. Each time I completed a sentence applause broke out in the first rows and with remarkable speed was taken up by all, to the very last brown shirt at the back of the room. Not one pair of hands insulted me by staying still. When my peroration had taken its full flight, followed by unusually prolonged clapping, I extricated myself from the mountain of flowers, with what dignity I could muster, and went to a seat which they showed me, in the front row beside Baldur von Schirach, youth-Führer, handsome as an opera tenor, while someone stood at the foot of the mountain of flowers and began to read an abridged translation of my speech, for the benefit of those young Nazis who, not knowing French, hadn't understood, but who had, none the less, applauded with irreproachable zeal.

I had developed a theme—agreed upon with A when he came to see me in Paris—which I called "Germanism and Latinity." I had treated it in a historico-philosophical way, well fitted to fascinate the German soul. I had tried to show—as I very sincerely believed—that our two nations throughout many centuries had

been the victims of a constantly renewed misunderstanding; that the misunderstanding had been
aggravated periodically by fitful withdrawals of
Germanism into itself, and had been attenuated, to
everyone's advantage, each time Germanism had consented, without too many mental reservations, to take
part in the Latin and Western civilization. In conclusion, I hoped that the surge of Germanic nationalism
we were witnessing, and trying to understand in spite
of certain aversions on matters of principle, would not
be an occasion for a bad-tempered withdrawal of German conscience into itself, but that, on the contrary,
Germanism would take the opportunity to discover
between itself and Latinity (of which France was
still the supreme representative) a harmony which
could seem neither suspect nor precarious, since it
would have been accepted by the most uncompromis-
ing element in Germanism.

As a French proverb states, flies aren't caught with
vinegar. I had tried to find the slant best calculated to
impress the audience favourably. But I knew I had
not curried favour by base flattery.

I then learned, while chatting with Baldur von
Schirach, that my audience had been made up long
beforehand, with the greatest care. The leaders of
youth organizations in some sixty regions—that is, in
almost all of Germany—had been brought there, and
when they went back were to call meetings of their

groups to repeat the main points of my speech. The seed I had sown was not likely to be wasted.

I was asked if I should like to spend the rest of the evening with some of the young leaders, picked from among the most interesting, so that I might talk to them in the absence of their elders, perfectly freely. It was far too tempting an opportunity to form my own opinion of the mysterious Nazi youth in whom, mainly, lay the future of Germany. I accepted willingly. Hermann joined them. On my way out with my new companions, as I took leave of A, that "pleasant civilian", with whom my adventure had originated, said to me, in a low voice:

"Pleased? It went well, didn't it? . . . You know no private individual has ever been received like this in Berlin."

My friend and former fellow-student, François-Poncet, the French Ambassador, shared this opinion and drew it to my attention, seasoning his real stupefaction with the banter taken for granted between two "archicubes" (as the alumni of the Ecole Normale Supérieure call themselves).

But I can feel that my readers want to interrupt to ask me two questions: "Why had the Nazis prepared such a reception for you?" and "What in heaven's name were you doing there in November 1934, with your ideas and your past?"

The first question is interesting because through it, in a limited but already characteristic case, we can lay a finger on the "Nazi mystery". True, even then the Nazis had no reputation for admiring thinkers and writers above all else; and my standing as a Frenchman and a "Leftist" was not, one would think, of a kind to provide me with additional testimonials. Yet, though there has always been a fundamental lack of reason in their movement, that has not been the case, as you know, in details; every one of their actions, even the most disconcerting, has always been motivated. What was the motivation in this case?

First there was my position, for so many years, in the eyes of the German public. My name was a familiar one, and that of a friend. It was known that I had shown understanding and sympathy for the German people at a time when they felt they were still under reprobation. They could remember a speech I had made at the Town Hall in Berlin, in 1925, before an immense crowd, when I had ended with the cry, in the name of the whole assembly: "We swear there shall never again be an army front between us." The year after, in the ex-Imperial Senate chamber, where all the political and intellectual élite of Berlin had gathered, I had made another speech entitled: "On the Way to Franco-German Friendship." That day Einstein came to me at the end of the meeting to grasp my hands. On many other occasions I had shown what value I attached to setting up a lasting and cordial peace between the two nations. The fact is that I had realized long since the evidence forced on us by history and geography: there will be no peace in Europe if there is not peace between France and Germany. The vow I spoke of in my introduction implied another: "I shall do everything to prevent another war between France and Germany."

When the Nazis came into power, they would have found it difficult to persuade the public—which did not yet take them at their word—that I was Germany's enemy, and it would have been impolitic to ostracize my name and my books. So they didn't try to. It was, on the contrary, clever of them to present me, in 1934, as their honoured guest. It was a way of saying: "You see, he sulked a little, out of loyalty to his old friends, but now he recognizes that we represent the real Germany." What's more, by receiving a writer with all that pomp, they indulged in the luxury, at little cost, of showing they weren't such enemies of culture as they were made out to be.

But there were other reasons, more immediate. The events in February 1934, of which I spoke in a previous chapter, had led me to assume for a while in France a role I had no desire to play. At the beginning of March I had given an important public lecture on "The Future of France", in which I tried to show that French people had no reason to fight one another,

158

and that instead of slipping rapidly into civil war, as they were doing, they would do better to attempt a rejuvenation and reconstruction of the country, not abandoning in the slightest the democratic ideal, but rather giving it greater reality and efficiency. I felt very clearly, even then, that the trouble, which might be mortal, with democracy, with all democracies, was on one hand the lack of accomplishment caused by unchecked excess of parliamentarianism and bureaucracy, on the other hand the lack of that pep and enthusiasm which gave totalitarian regimes the illusory advantage of apparently representing the youth and future of the world. And I was firmly convinced that to preserve fundamental liberties it was no longer sufficient to fight Fascism negatively, and that democracy itself must be made an ever new and exciting goal, always situated in the future and capable of firing all hearts.

At the end of my speech, in which they saw the program of a new era, the representatives of almost all the youth groups in politics, even those most completely opposed to each other, had come to me and asked me to help them draw up a plan for a general Reform of France, which all the groups they came from would then support, and which would soon impose itself on a bewildered Parliament. Their aim was clear, and so was the call to duty. The most immediate task was to prevent Frenchmen from fighting in the streets, in encounters which would be far more bloody than the night of February 6. Now the very men who might organize such fights and lead their groups to assault against one another were going to meet several times a week and work peacefully under my direction. So it came about that the leader of the *Croix de Feu* volunteers and the leader of the "Young Patriot" volunteers were included in my group. Seated opposite them at the same table would be the young leaders of trade-unionism, socialism, radicalism. . . . If these men didn't fight, there could be no fight; for it wasn't the old men in each group who would be the first out in the streets. I had civil war under lock and key, for several months. And that in itself was something.

Our far-reaching, more distant objective was to give France a new constitution, born of the old, identically the same in its republican spirit and in its absolute respect for the Rights of Man, but freed from some defects and better adapted to modern needs; in a word, more dynamic—a constitution youth would love and defend with energy because it had created it.

That was what was called "the July 9th movement". The plan for the Reform of France in which our efforts culminated was, in fact, published on that date in 1934, with the title: "The July 9th Plan".

Personally, I had no desire whatsoever to take on broader political responsibilities. My inclination was to remain a free writer. I intended to stay at the head of the movement only so long as was strictly necessary; in other words, so long as there was acute danger of civil war, or of a Fascist *coup d'état* (or even, what wasn't out of the question, the threat of a double *coup d'état* carried out by the extremists—Communists and Fascists—with its consequent appalling confusion). The minute I felt that danger averted, I would let the organization we had created function by itself, and go back to my own work. But people found it hard to believe that I was so disinterested; many ascribed vast ambitions to me—with no tinge of blame. And that accounted for the very curious advances made to me by certain people. One day, as I have stated, it was the chief of General Weygand's personal staff who brought me a plan concerning the army. Another day an influential Senator, who had been Minister many times, asked me if I would authorize him to start within the Senate itself a group destined to assure the triumph of the July 9th ideas: "We number about twenty already, quite determined," he said to me. I was offered newspapers already in existence, and proposals were made me for the creation of newspapers I should control. Bankers offered to raise funds. Some ministers in power in the Doumergue government let me understand, or told me openly, that for the time being they must lend themselves to the mediocre policy of their leader, but that when the time came, I could count on them (particularly one of them, whom I saw, with some amusement, become Minister again after a long eclipse, under the Pétain government). The Premier himself, the former President of the Republic, Doumergue, when he received people, ostentatiously displayed on his table the July 9th Plan, and tried to introduce fragments of it into the Project for a Reform of the Constitution he made great show of having under way. But the zeal, or rather visions, of my partisans did not stop at that. Things of this kind were said to me: "Each country has its own style. . . . If France is some day to have a dictator, naturally he'll be an intellectual—a writer. . . ." And they watched closely, to catch the nuance of my smile. I couldn't explain to them that I was as averse to the dictatorship one wields as to that one suffers, and moreover, even if I could have it by just lifting my little finger, I'd take good care not to exchange my free life as a writer for the terrible life of "leaders of men". They wouldn't have believed me. When my group of young co-workers met, for convenience' sake, in a café or bar, one of them, a socialist engineer named Vallon, had got into the habit of shouting as a joke, when I entered the room: "Gentlemen! the Führer!" . . . Thank heavens, it was only a poor joke. But it could fall safely on innocent ears.

The Nazis, as usual, were well aware of this through their agents and emissaries. Since, following their own psychology, they couldn't imagine such lack of ambition; since, on the other hand, given their own experience, they knew it was not prudent in troubled times to say beforehand where any man or movement might stop, they saw no great risk in treating me as one of the possible leaders—if not the leader—of the France of tomorrow; and it was to that eventual figure —which I alone knew would never come to life—more than to the writer, that they dedicated the mountain of flowers and the Wagnerian horns.

As for me, when I accepted their invitation, I had had to overcome deep-rooted repugnance. I had no wish to talk with their Germany. But when, in the past, I had made my vow to oppose war, I knew quite well, as I said, that the danger of war in Europe was primarily the danger of war between France and Germany; and that if we must one day make a supreme effort to divert that peril, we should surely not be faced, on that day, with a friendly Germany, or a German government moved by human and generous ideas. Since we hadn't succeeded—in part through our own fault, through hers, through that of others—in turning republican Germany into a sincere and firm friend and in saving her from the schemes of her internal enemies; since we had let Nazism eat into her bit by bit—and it was not a question of eradicating the disease by the surgery of preventive war—it was necessary in 1934 to consider Nazi Germany as a fact, an established and confirmed fact. Besides, even if resort to force had not been opposed to all we had believed in and advocated for fifteen years, it had in the meantime become more costly and more hazardous. France, deeply divided in 1934, was not capable of waging war without risking a sudden internal rupture. No more was Europe, as I saw it. What bade fair to come from war was general disorder, from which only Soviet Russia might benefit; that is to say, the transformation of a war of nations into a medley of civil wars, and, in the end, total ruin of the West.

In other words, in 1934 especially, no really satisfactory line of action could be envisaged. There was room only for a makeshift policy, a waiting game. And the greater the responsibilities I had taken, or might be led to take, in the affairs of my country, the smaller my right to deal with the question in the abstract. When I undertook this journey, I said to myself: "I must form my own opinion, at first hand, of the Nazis, leaders and men. And, in so far as I am able, I must prevent the occurrence of new mistakes, and the creation of situations which we'd have all the trouble in the world putting straight."

Therefore I lent myself willingly to the contacts arranged for me with the young Nazis. I spent with them not only the evening after my lecture, but many other moments in the following days. As several of them had become my bodyguards, they accompanied me in my outings, waited for me when I called on some official, and chatted with me as we went about. In the evening, around beer-mugs in some tavern, they sang their songs, some of which, incidentally, were simple and beautiful, and with a peculiar edge of revolt against the old Germany of wealth and of nobility. They spoke to me with open hearts; and I have no right to doubt their sincerity, for their guilelessness was stamped on their faces. They spoke of their lives in the S.S. or S.A., and of the special charm it had for them. "Do you know why we like this uniform?" they'd say. "Because it erases all social differences among us. See that fellow over there, who just sang? He's just a tramway operator in Thuringia. When his work is done, he joins his pals, some of whom are sons of well-to-do bourgeois. He is their equal. . . . He's even the superior of most of them, because he has a rank." So I realized that even under the Republic, the common man in the street in Germany had always felt a certain painful lack of democratic equality, not so much under the law as in daily life; and that one source of strength for the new regime was that it satisfied that feeling, though in an unexpected way. They also said (it was obviously a lesson taught them, but it contributed to their satisfaction): "We are really true democrats—much more so than the Italian Fascists, for example. In Italy Fascism is, at bottom, an aristocratic organization. Everything comes from above. Here everything springs from the mass and rises to the Führer." I didn't argue, as you may well imagine. I was out to learn. I contrived, with precaution, to make them speak of the great leaders, of the Führer himself. About their great leaders they seemed divided. The name of Goebbels brought smiles. Rudolf Hess was perhaps the only one to claim all sympathies. But what most interested them was their own leader, Baldur von Schirach, and even more the Supreme Leader, the Führer. They placed him at a level entirely apart, above all rivalry and quarrels, in the light of serenity and infallibility. I alluded to the recent massacres of June 30, 1934, whose incomplete and darkly veiled story had sent a thrill of horror throughout the West. I gathered that several of my young Nazis—probably of proletarian origin, who had grown up in socialistic or even communistic families—had a certain leaning towards the advanced elements in the party that Röhm, the principal victim on June 30, was supposed to represent. But even for them the Führer's act was above argument. "We consider," said one, calmly, "that the Führer holds in his hands all the powers of the people, delegated by them to him; and more especially the power of justice. In ordinary cases he does not act himself. But he has a perfect right to do so if he judges it urgent and requisite for the safety of the people. He delivers the sentence and executes it in the name of the people. When he went 'down there' in haste, to punish Röhm, he did just that." And you felt that it wouldn't have taken much to make him add: "We must thank our Führer for having taken on such a job, instead of leaving it to the judges and the executioner."

I felt them out on the Jewish question, confessing that the Jewish persecutions were deeply disturbing to us morally and were harming the prestige of the new regime abroad. They answered with embarrassment and moderation. They quoted statistics showing that Jews had taken a really exaggerated place in very important professions, vital to society. But they seemed not to profess the extreme doctrines of anti-Semitism, nor did they incline to accept responsibility for the brutality to which certain elements in the party had been led.

I tried to tackle them on the subject of liberty. I wanted to know if they hadn't kept a kind of longing for it. The one I called Hermann answered in these words: "I don't need to be free against the *Vaterland*. I need to feel the *Vaterland* is quite free, yes; then I too shall feel I am quite free. . . ." At that moment the look in his eyes was very pure, the loyalty in his face was charming (the face of a young sixteenth-century priest, perfectly ready to die, but also perfectly ready to have some hundred heretics roasted, so that the Church could feel "quite free").

They themselves asked me many questions about France, in which they were greatly interested. Two of them had canoed on our rivers in the east; another had hiked there; but seemingly without establishing any real contact with the country. There was wonderful naïveté in their information about France: "What a pity," sighed one of them, "that so lovely a country should be Negroid to such an extent!" Quite astounded, restraining a laugh, I answered that we in France had no colour prejudices, and that in many of our colonies there were large populations, black or mixed in breed, with whom we couldn't be on better terms; that in the mother country, too, Negroes were most welcome and well treated, but that in fact there were very few of them, and even fewer mulattoes; and that in Paris, for instance, you could very easily walk around in the streets for an hour without meeting a single one. They found it hard to believe me.

But more than anything they wanted to hear about French youth, its aspirations, how it regarded the future, and especially the future of Franco-German relations.

They had been told that I was the "leader of French political youth"; and that perhaps I'd soon be something more. So they placed me, in their imaginations, somewhere between a youth-Führer—like Baldur von Schirach—and an actual Führer in embryo. You can see with what respect my words were greeted, and what far-reaching echoes they were likely to have among the youth of the entire Reich.

I took advantage of that to assure them that French youth had no hatred for Germany—that was truth itself; that the reasonable aspirations of Germany would meet with no opposition from them; that their only desire was to work in peace to build a new France; that therefore, if the dangers of war should rise between the two countries, it could only come from Germany's return to its old imperialistic dreams. My young Nazis declared that the imperialism of the old Empire was absolutely dead. Hitler's nationalism did not revive it in any way, was even opposed to it in essence. For, they explained, with great insistence, the imperialism of a William II consisted in a desire to extend German domination over nations who were not German; whereas, on the contrary, National Socialism aimed only at uniting all men of German blood, rejecting extraneous elements.

These conversations on Franco-German relations with the young Nazi rank and file did not prevent me from seeing A, that cordial fellow, several times a day. He helped me to make my appointments, gave me useful advice, told me of what people I should be wary. But, above all, he let me see more clearly into the underground workings of the regime and into his own thoughts.

Now I must tell you about him a little more, and first say how I met him.

In the early autumn one of the members of the managing committee for the July 9th movement, one of the most distinguished and active, Jean Thomas, had said to me:

"I have a request to pass on to you. It comes from a German whom someone introduced to me, a young man of my generation who seems very likable. He's been active for some time now in the movement which is taking shape among French and German youth: intellectual interchange, mutual visits, and so on. His name is Otto Abetz. He isn't a Nazi; but naturally he can work only by taking the Nazis into account and not setting them against him. Quite recently he organized the trip of a young French group into Germany; they had a remarkably warm welcome everywhere; even the local authorities took part in it. . . . Now he'd like to come here with some young Germans, very few, belonging to intellectual circles, and he wants us to receive them, in a simple manner. For example, we might call a private July 9th meeting, to which we'd ask some sixty of our young comrades, carefully picked. For that I could lend the room used by the Centre de Documentation Sociale . . ." (Thomas directed the Centre de Documentation Sociale, quartered in one of the buildings of the École Normale Supérieure). "You would preside at the meeting, which would consist in an exchange of questions between the young Germans and any members of the audience who took the floor. Abetz understands very well that, given the state of mind in France, we can't manage for him anything like the fancy receptions they give over there to our young people . . . it's a question of national temperament. But if he is to go on with his work, he must be able to say back home: 'You see, in France there's beginning to be a response. . . .' And if that response takes place under the auspices of the July 9th movement, to which the Germans attach great importance, then it'll mean ten times more to them. In any case, we'll please Abetz that way."

I had consented. The meeting had been held. Everything took place in a proper and even cordial way. The young Frenchmen united by the July 9th Plan had no basic hostility against Germany. They wanted to work and not to wage war. They hoped that a broad collaboration could be established between the two countries. But even among the Rightist youth groups there was little sympathy for Nazi ideology, and open aversion for some of the methods used by the regime and for excesses of which it was guilty within. So, without wishing to meddle in their neighbours' affairs, the young men grouped around me welcomed the chance to put some questions to their German visitors and get some light on the matter, if possible. Our guests submitted with fairly good grace and stood the test cleverly. They took the position, on the whole, of ascribing excesses under the regime to the inevitable reaction against excesses under previous regimes, or against abuses which had arisen to the detriment of public welfare; and they left the impression that, given time, things would settle down. I must add that in our desire to avoid all causes of misunderstanding between them and us, we were inclined to be easily satisfied. Perhaps on our part this was a form of culpable complacency. But let those who have never sacrificed any clear-sightedness to their love of peace throw the first stone.

On their side, the young Germans put a few questions to our July 9th group, and seemed satisfied with the answers.

To thank me for this meeting which had gratified all his desires, Otto Abetz had come to see me himself; and during the remainder of his stay we had had several private talks. I had a liking for the man. First, he was cheerful. And I have a weakness; I like cheerful men. In appearance he was a healthy fellow, with reddish hair, an open freckled face with frank, clear-cut features, a pleasant voice, often interrupted by laughter. He might very well have come from French Flanders or Alsace. He described to me his youth and adolescence. He represented himself as a real western German who by all his natural affinities and cultural tradition felt a bond with the western nations. The Belgians, the northern French, the Swiss, they were his brothers. On the other hand, he felt nothing but aversion and mistrust towards the Prussians, whom he held responsible for the misfortunes of Germany and the mistaken course she had followed since the eighteenth century. In his eyes the Prussians were to be counted among those damned Eastern populations who have never appeared in Europe without bringing it disorder and destruction. They had succeeded in filtering through into western Germany, taking the best positions there and ruling as masters, and even in corrupting it by infecting it with their mentality. They had contributed more than anyone else to raising between France and Germany the absurd wall of hatred against which the best forces in the West had crashed, and which was the main obstacle to a harmonious reconstruction of Europe.

Otto Abetz told me that as a vocation he had chosen to be a painter (he too!); that he had studied at a Fine Arts School in the Grand Duchy of Baden and begun a modest career as an artist; but the problems of the time had haunted him to the point of destroying his serenity of mind; and he realized that he would find solace only if he devoted himself to them, or at least to the one which seemed most urgent and dramatic to him: the problem of reconciling the West, which was in reality the Franco-German problem. He had first worked at knowing France thoroughly; he had studied its literature, travelled in its provinces. He had done more: he had married a Frenchwoman, from the vicinity of Lille. Their child, a little boy, was the very symbol of the union his father dreamed of seeing consummated one day between the two nations, which, in fact, he had made his aim in life.

All this, confided to me in the most simple way, was enough to claim my sympathy. It would have taken a very hard heart to suspect him of lying. It was as though I was listening to a German translation of my own past dreams. Had I myself been born on the other side of the Rhine, it seemed to me, I couldn't have spoken otherwise. I was therefore only the more eager to find out what the secret feelings of such a man might be when faced with the Nazi rise to power; and especially what his attitude towards them was at the moment, what part of his dream he still thought he could preserve. Did the mission he had given himself still make sense, now that they were there?

He answered me in evasive and cautious formulas, which nevertheless let his thought show clearly. It was evident, as he talked, that he was not a Nazi, and even that he would have wished for his country a quite different political orientation. But if you wish to act and not merely to dream, things must be taken as they are. What merit would there be, anyway, if circumstances were the way one would like them? The

Nazis, he seemed to say, are the outcome of mistakes accumulated by lots of people. You mustn't be too hard on them. Their good point is that, not knowing exactly where they came from, they don't know much better where they're going. Their ideas don't matter much, for at bottom they haven't any. They're a blind force, a sort of large storm-cloud which will last just so long. It would be ideal if we could direct its course so that, as it crosses the skies of Germany, and of Europe, it does not cause irreparable disaster; and, in fact, so that quite unconsciously it accomplishes something useful—a hope that is not absurd. Everything will depend on the intelligence with which clear-sighted people, inside as well as outside, will deal with this blind phenomenon.

You realize that Abetz did not spread these views before me in the dangerously straightforward manner I have used. He slipped them in deftly, through short humorous sentences, sly implications; and the laughter and good-tempered sallies he mingled with his explanations helped to make them quite acceptable. I myself had expressed somewhat similar views in a series of articles on Germany published by the *Dépêche de Toulouse* a year before. Trying, for instance, to answer the question: "What does Germany want?" I said: "It's not so much what she wants that matters as what she will want; and it's partly up to us to bring her to want certain things and not to want certain others." So I was prepared to see in Abetz's words more than just a means of evasion.

"It comes to this," he said ingratiatingly, helping himself out with his optimistic laugh, "we have devoted ourselves to the same cause, you and I: that of preserving peace, and at the point where it is most threatened, between France and Germany; and we have found the same obstacle in our way, or the same puzzle: the Nazi phenomenon. As for you, you're on the outside; but I'm inside it. . . . We must manage to work along the same lines, in touch with each other. . . . You can count on me." He made an allusion to those "men of good will" in my novel who dream of working for peace, here and there, making use of a network of secret intrigue. "Imagine one of them in my place," he said to me, "and you'll understand my position very clearly."

I really thought I understood it clearly. Without making too much of it, he gave me some indications of the method he had adopted to "work from the inside". On the one hand, he had tried to organize a system of exchange between the young people of France and Germany, which had a double advantage: it was useful work and it gave him, personally, a little start towards importance. On the other hand, he had sought out the means to exercise some central influence, by securing the confidence of one of the powerful men in the regime. This was too much in keeping with my idea of "action on vital points" for me not to be struck by it. The person he had chosen was von Ribbentrop.

Ribbentrop had not yet a really official situation. He was only the head of the Ribbentrop-büro, that is, a kind of laboratory for research and experiment in foreign policy. But his influence was already quite important, and his aim, which he did not hide from his intimate co-workers, was to become the head of the Wilhelmstrasse.

"He's still very little known here," Abetz said to me. "He has no really official position. . . . But he's a rising star. . . . You'll see. He's one of the most intelligent among them—in my opinion the most intelligent and by a long way. He has no prejudices. He's about as much of a Nazi as I am. . . . He knows France very well; he used to live here. . . . He has no basic hostility towards her; on the contrary. . . . In short, I'm betting on him. He has accepted my services. . . . I hope to make myself indispensable little by little."

In a last interview Abetz had asked me to come to lecture in Berlin. "You'll be serving the good cause," he said. Because of the very risk involved, the proposal attracted me. We searched for a subject which would be neither too dangerous nor too insignificant.

"You might," suggested Abetz, "draw their attention to that idea of the West and the union of Europe around the West which is close to both our hearts. . . . Show them that they'll never find their way if they draw apart from the Latin world, and from France especially, as many advise them."

"Right," I answered half jokingly. "I'll speak to them about Charlemagne—for, after all, Charlemagne was a gentleman who understood about the West, and he had found a solution to the problem. . . . As your compatriots have a liking for vast historical perspectives, I'll explain to them that their misfortunes come, not, as they believe, from the Treaty of Versailles, but from the Treaty of Verdun, the one in 843 which sanctioned the division of the western Empire and the final separation between the Germans and French."

"Marvellous!" Abetz exclaimed gaily. "You have no idea how well you've hit it. Just at present at home Charlemagne is in the bad graces of a whole clique whose influence must be counteracted. Now's the time to rehabilitate Charlemagne! Yes, that's it! In Germany, you know, you must impress people with grand ideas; go back to the Flood if you have to. Let's rehabilitate Charlemagne!"

We had parted on this keynote of sense and good humour.

Once during my stay in Berlin (we were at the time, I remember, in an alcove of one of the lounges in the Hotel Adlon, on the ground floor, and he spoke in a low voice) he spoke to me of the June 30th massacres.

"Yes, the execution was terrible," he said to me. "But don't think Hitler acted without reason. If he had not struck with such extraordinary promptness and energy, anything might have happened. A real plot was hatched by the most disturbing elements in the party . . . the thing was well under way. One of my friends witnessed by chance a gathering of storm-troopers, in the dead of night, at crossroads in a forest. . . . Those men were on the way to join Röhm and the others at an appointed spot. . . . They were perhaps the best of the storm-troopers. . . . In a few more hours it would have been too late."

As Abetz said all this in a low voice, I could see that crossroads at night in the German forest, the bands of armed men coming from different paths and exchanging their signs of recognition . . . outlaws, ready to kill, as easily for one leader as for another. It had a strong mediæval quality.

Abetz concluded:

"Luckily, in such cases Hitler has lightning reactions. He didn't hesitate one second. He jumped into his plane and annihilated the plot at one blow, by crushing it at the very head. . . ."

I hinted cautiously that perhaps it was an excellent thing indeed for Hitler, and for those who had linked their fortunes to his; but that I was somewhat astonished that he, Abetz, who was not a Nazi, should seem so clearly delighted over it. . . . Suppose the plot of Röhm and his satellites had succeeded, would it not have started a war of mutual extermination between the Nazis, and thus forecast Germany's liberation?

Abetz shook his head.

"No," he declared, showing no desire to explain more fully, "it could only have brought about the worst. . . . The men behind Röhm were the most violent and the most dangerous."

He added with a smothered laugh:

"It's a great pity Hitler didn't kill them all!"

It was hard for me to drag from him as complete an elucidation as I wished. He obviously preferred not to make his disclosures too categorically precise; I did not wish to give the impression of submitting him to a cross-examination. I managed, however, little by little to get a notion of the way he saw the *Nazi mystery* from inside, and I can sum it up as follows:

In that still chaotic vortex, full of obscure possibilities, the Party, there were two main tendencies. One attracted the fanatics, the out-and-out adventurers, the sanguinary brutes, capable of anything, who didn't give a damn for German and Occidental civilization. The other drew relatively reasonable people who saw in Nazism a way for Germany to make over her interior organization and to regain her place in Europe, but who'd just as soon see the regime tone down gradually and find a peaceful *modus vivendi* with the Western powers. "For men devoted as we are to peace and reconciliation," Abetz said persuasively, "there can be no doubt: the first of these tendencies means catastrophe; the second, a sound chance for peaceful collaboration; therefore we must hope the second will triumph." (Abetz apparently didn't consider getting rid of both.) Röhm had represented the first tendency; he was dead, but it wasn't. As it had not succeeded in gaining the upper hand by violence, it might try to achieve its ends through intrigue, winning over the Führer after having tried to overthrow him. As for the reasonable tendency, it was represented by von Ribbentrop more forcefully and lucidly than by anyone else. . . . That's why Abetz in his search for a point of central action had chosen him. The more von Ribbentrop's importance grew, the stronger the chances for peace.

And Alfred Rosenberg, on which side must we place him? Abetz answered with an evasive grimace. Probably Rosenberg wasn't the worst of the lot, personally, but he had helped to supply the party with some of its myths, the most dangerous and the best fitted to inflame fanaticism with regard to race, blood, and other nonsense. Moreover, in his position as Big Boss of Foreign Affairs, he was the principal obstacle to the rise of Ribbentrop. And Goebbels, that dark, feverish little man? Abetz now answered with a smile. He seemed, without saying so, to regard Goebbels as a barker in a side-show, about whom one doesn't ask too anxiously what he thinks or doesn't think. With him things would always come out all right. But the Führer himself? I queried. Wasn't he the one whose secret inclinations towards adventure and war or towards reasonable issues it was most important to be sure of? Abetz became doubly cautious. But he intimated that the execution of Röhm could be taken as an indication.

The fact is that in Abetz's remarks, as in those of my young Nazi leaders, Hitler appeared enthroned above a cloud, immersed in reverie, a little absent-minded with regard to men and things below, perhaps even rather uncertain about the value of these men and things and about the decisions it would be best to make concerning them. He was a puzzle to the observer because he was a puzzle to himself. It could be said of him above all others that he'd want whatever he was made to want by circumstances and by the tact, or lack of tact, of those around him. It was in him that the opposing potentialities of Nazi Germany were concentrated, because they happened to correspond marvellously with his own indeterminate nature. Therefore it was essential to arrange a permanent system of influences around him. Ribbentrop had already gained his confidence but in a manner which was not exclusive and which afforded no contact with the diplomatic personnel. Our aim would be reached only with the establishment of Ribbentrop as master in the Wilhelmstrasse, when all the diplomatic apparatus would be in his hands, and the future before him. By procuring successes for Ribbentrop, you increased his credit with the Führer and worked for the good cause.

Abetz gave me another mark of friendship by taking me home with him. He occupied one floor of a small house, in a new development on the outskirts of Berlin, surrounded by gardens. There were few rooms, small, and most scantily furnished. I saw no maid. Madame Abetz, the Frenchwoman from Lille, was a slight, rather pale woman, with something in her look, in her voice, that was humble and valiant, fervent and tender. They seemed closely united. In their small apartment the two of them reminded me of those couples of poor young artists or intellectuals, who live at Montparnasse or in the neighbourhood of the Parc-Montsouris, supported by their faith. They showed me their little boy, a good, lovingly reared child. And it's true I found him touching, born as he was, not of a chance meeting between two people, but of an ideal which had drawn them together.

At one point Abetz was called to the telephone. He came back saying:

"They need me over there. . . ." ("Over there" was an office for foreign relations with which he was connected, and which I suppose worked under Ribbentrop.) "But it'll take me only a few minutes. You can wait for me here. My wife will keep you company."

Madame Abetz, left alone with me and the child, spoke of her husband with tender admiration:

"He has given himself entirely to the cause of bringing our two countries together. I've done my best to help him. He is so enthusiastic and generous by nature! He left the small position he held to devote himself entirely to this task, for of course all his time must be free, to see people, and to travel if need be. So we found ourselves with no resources whatever. He absolutely refused to receive money for that work —lest anyone insinuate that he was doing it in his own interest. So I had to borrow money from my family in France. That's how we've lived—modestly as you see. Even now that he's working with Ribbentrop and being very useful to him, he won't accept even the smallest salary. . . . He consents at most to having his travelling expenses refunded, for otherwise you can see it would be impossible."

Her eyes ablaze with some inner fire, she told me this, beside her little boy, there in that apartment, like a needy student's. And it was said to me by a young Frenchwoman, in my own language! It would have taken abnormal suspicion not to be gripped by emotion, not to believe what was said.

VI

THE MYSTERY OF
RIBBENTROP AND CO.

THE PARTICULAR PROBLEM which in the autumn of
1934, at the time of my stay in Berlin, conditioned
the next future of Franco-German relations was the
problem of the Saar. You may remember that the
Saar territory had been put, by an article of the
Treaty of Versailles, in a temporary situation which
had to be resolved after fifteen years by a plebiscite.
According to the results of this plebiscite, the Saar
would be tied definitely to France or to Germany,
or even could become an independent state, under
the control of the League of Nations. The plebiscite's operations had to take place under the control
of the French civil and military power, since it was
France which held the territory, as decided by the
treaty.

I had worked on this problem before leaving Paris. The time set by the Treaty of Versailles for the plebiscite was approaching. I had had, in particular, a long talk with the General Secretary of the Quai d'Orsay, Alexis Léger, who, because of his permanent office, would, I thought, play a more effective part in the development of the question than a minister destined to disappear from one day to the next. I told him that, as I saw it, we should give in to the advances made by Germany, who offered compensations to be discussed, in exchange for our giving back the Saar, purely and simply, without a plebiscite.

"Even should such compensations not be very considerable," I maintained, "though they may be, they'll be better than nothing. And in my opinion, if we insist on the plebiscite, more than 80 per cent of the votes will be against us; the only outcome for us will be a crying failure, and we'll have provided Germany with a proof of ill will and an inflammatory anti-French topic. . . . Let's not renew the mistake we've made so many times, of giving in too late, crossly and without profit, when we could have made a good trade earlier, smilingly at that." Léger retorted: "According to my information, Hitler will poll a bare 60 per cent of the votes. The failure will be his, morally. It'll be the first disavowal of his politics that he has had to face. We have no right to spare him anything." I replied that the calculation seemed to me false at every point, but that I had no way of proving that Hitler would carry 80 or 85 per cent of the votes, and not 55 or 60 per cent.

In Berlin my friend François-Poncet, the French Ambassador, disclosed to me other aspects of the question. In the first phase the Germans had asked us to give up the plebiscite, which bothered and annoyed them, in exchange for certain compensations to be determined (perhaps rectifying the frontier to our advantage, or certain rights over the mine production, economic agreements, and so on). We had refused. Then the Germans said: "Since you want the plebiscite element, we'll keep it but give it another character. Let's come to complete agreement on a settlement of the Saar question beforehand; then we'll ask the population to pronounce on the agreement. It will do so almost unanimously. So the plebiscite, instead of registering a Franco-German split, will on the contrary confirm the agreement and be a success for the two governments."

"And we didn't accept?" I exclaimed. "But it's madness. For my part, I'm convinced the Germans exaggerate the risk they run in the plebiscite provided for in the treaty; that in fact it'll be a success for them. But if they're afraid of it and want to take out insurance against it, so much the better for us. And so much the better, too, for the future relations between the two nations if, instead of creating a new occasion for bitterness between them, we create even a semblance of good feeling."

"That's exactly what I think," said François-Poncet, "but, as you know, it's not the first time my advice has been overruled."

I had to try to patch up the situation and, above all, to grasp clearly the thought, even the hidden thought of the masters of Germany.

I had several interviews, the two most important with Rosenberg and Goebbels. Rosenberg remained the supreme originator and adviser in matters of foreign policy. Ribbentrop's influence, though already quite important, was exercised only behind the scenes. Besides, he wasn't in Berlin at that time. I knew I'd find him back in Paris and had been assured by Abetz that no obstacles would come from his end.

With Rosenberg as with Goebbels, we reached the problem of the Saar only after what communiqués call a "vast survey of the horizon." Rosenberg ruled over an edifice which, without having the name, looked rather like a ministry in reduction. He received me in an office, itself unassuming in size and scantily furnished. These men hadn't quite settled in yet. They still had some characteristics of an army of occupation.

In front of me sat a middle-aged man, rather thin, quite unexceptionally Nordic in type, the kind one is as apt to find in the Scandinavian countries and Great

Britain as in the northern European plain. He spoke distinctly. He was direct, not particularly cordial, but evoking no antagonism. We came to rapid agreement on the idea that there were no insoluble problems in Europe, not even very intricate ones, and their apparent intricacy stemmed mainly from those who handled them: diplomats, bureaucrats, old-style politicians. He complained about the Doumergue government's attitude towards Germany, and specifically about the new "encirclement" Barthou had outlined just before his tragic death—Barthou, the perfect type of the old-style politician, according to Rosenberg. Anyway, not one of the problems left hanging was worth a war to solve it. Was Rosenberg sincere in what he said? I don't know, even now. But he hit upon a striking formula: "If we were foolish enough to wage war against each other, then it's the little Mongol horses who'd come to graze among the ruins of Europe."

Rosenberg admitted that the only question still pending between France and Germany was that of the Saar.

"It's a pity," he said, "you insisted so much on the plebiscite. You're going to have troubles on your hands. Suppose disturbances spring up over there. You never can tell. . . . People are wrought up. You'd have to check them, your troops. . . . And suppose blood flowed? . . . We'd have a lot of difficulties preventing our people from acting up. . . . From one step to the next, no one can tell where it might end. And you won't play the hero's part. There's surely some way of finding a better solution."

And he referred to a plan which had already been mentioned to me: to ask French authorities in the Saar not to be in the foreground at the time of the plebiscite, and even to appear uninterested in the operation. To place the control, and the responsibility of maintaining order, in the hands of a mixed group of war veterans, half French, half German, chosen among the leaders of the large organizations. "They are men with self-control, used to dealing with other such situations. Their presence will be a guarantee of impartiality and will be enough to keep the people calm. I'm sure not a move will be made. But let's suppose the worst—that they should feel things got out of hand. Well—they would appeal, in due form, to the occupying army to restore order, precisely to the extent they would specify. You will have taken no initiative. No responsibility can fall back on you."

"That interests me very much," I answered. "I'll think it over. . . . Do you authorize me, if need be, to present this to the French government as a plan assured beforehand of your approval?"

"Absolutely. In any case, Dr. Goebbels will speak to you about it also, and Chancellor Hitler too, if you see him."

Goebbels did receive me the following Monday. I had been told, the day before, that if I really wished to see the Führer-Chancellor, himself, I must prolong my stay by at least forty-eight hours, as he had left Berlin for Munich, if I remember rightly, and wouldn't be back till Wednesday afternoon. I should have gone to that interview with great curiosity. But imperative reasons prevented me from putting off my departure till then. I was scheduled, in fact, to speak in Strasbourg and Nancy on the ideas of the July 9th Plan.

Goebbels received me with a great show of heartiness. He asked me straight off to speak German, as that would make it easier for him. He declared without preamble:

"I know you'd have liked to see the Führer. And it would really have been a good thing. But I hear you can't possibly stay long enough for that. He is very sorry himself. I saw him before he left. We discussed at length the conversation I was to have with you. So that"—and Goebbels emphasized the words—"you can consider all I'm going to say exactly as if it came from his very lips."

He spoke of my lecture, having read the reviews of it:

"You see how the Berlin papers played it up? And it was the same all over Germany. . . ."

He spoke about my stay in Berlin, seeming to know all its details, about France of the moment, the part

I played, and the good fortune it would be for her if men like me replaced professional politicians. He, too, sneered at professional politicians of the old school, at those men terribly warped by their profession, he said, who have lost the habit of seeing reality and feed on words, who are incapable of solving problems, but complicate them at will, making of them matters for litigation.

"Most of them began as lawyers, anyway. It's not the fundamental issues that interest them, it's the quibbling they raise around them."

It took no great effort of courtesy on my part to acquiesce. For since the events in February, faced by the display of impotence the parliamentary world continued to give us, I was going through a stage of severity with regard to professional politicians.

Goebbels warmed up to his subject. I could recognize the very dark, thin, almost puny little man, nervous, almost feverish—just as his portraits showed him. Though he remained seated, he stretched out his chest and neck when talking, like an orator who, standing, tries to dominate a crowd. He had moreover many of the tricks of the orator—in gesture, intonation, and stringing together of sentences. His voice, his eyes gave out fire. His conviction might not be deep, but it was well acted. I thought: "After all, I'd like to be told about democracy, liberty, international justice, the fraternity of all men, with as much enthusiasm."

He, too, said how desirous Germany was to live in peace with her neighbours, particularly with France.

"We've only the question of the Saar, now, to eliminate. . . ."

On the Saar problem he used, in the main, Rosenberg's arguments, but weighted with more vehemence. He insisted a great deal on the dangers to which France would expose herself gratuitously if she took charge of policing the plebiscite. He drew a vivid picture of possible events:

"The Saar is full of Communist agitators. Who can prevent them from starting a fight? Our partisans will retort. . . . And then, if your soldiers step in and fire, if German blood flows, how can I prevent intense emotion from sweeping over Germany? A war may originate without either you or us wanting it, by a mere inflation of a local disorder. . . . It would be perfectly absurd. That's what must be prevented!"

And in the name of the Führer he confirmed the fact that the plan to place the control and policing of the plebiscite in the hands of the leaders of war veterans in both countries would be greeted with favour by the Reich government.

I had done some thinking since my talk with Rosenberg. I was still thinking while listening to Goebbels (and to Hitler through Goebbels). I kept repeating to myself: "Where's the pitfall under all this?" And

193

I was on the lookout for a pitfall. But, in all honesty, I couldn't manage to find one. I couldn't see what possible harm France could suffer if she accepted the proposed procedure. I answered Goebbels:

"The idea seems reasonable and human to me. It presents our two peoples with an occasion for contact—in fact, a chivalrous one—the effect of which I trust will be excellent for the future. I'll try to get the French government to accept it."

Those who are on close terms with the devil maintain that he sometimes has good ideas, but they must be snatched hastily, as he's easily discouraged. Perhaps that day the Nazis really had a good idea; or an angel had prompted them. . . .

Five and a half years later, I still have not discovered what possible treachery could cloak itself in their plan for a commission of war veterans. True, I have no persecution complex, and have sinned more than once in my life through excess of trustfulness.

When I took the train back at the Berlin station, the last hand I shook was the one of Abetz. He called after me: "See you soon! In Paris!"

After my interview with Goebbels we had had a long conversation, Abetz and I.

"I find very interesting this idea of having the Saar plebiscite controlled by a commission of war veterans," I had said to him; "as it seems to me no reasonable objection can be brought against it, and as, on the other hand, I see in it an opportunity for our two countries to fraternize, through some of their finest elements and in a situation where, on the contrary, they might have clashed with acrimony, I'll do all I can to get the French government's consent to the plan. If necessary I'll get public opinion behind it. But you know what governments are. Even when they can find no objection in principle to confront you with, they fall back on difficulties in execution. . . . And if they don't, the important civil servants in their entourage do. . . . And if such difficulties don't arise of themselves, they invent them. That's a part of the 'inefficiency complex' of civil servants; and the older the service, the more prevalent it is. You can well see that this plan has every characteristic guaranteed to displease them: it is direct, unconventional, contrary to all precedent; it makes all kinds of red tape useless from the start; it tends to suggest the terrible idea that, in some cases, a few decent fellows can control situations out of which chancelleries make mountains. . . . So I must be able to nip in the bud all the spiteful manœuvres and sabotage that I foresee, by saying: 'This plan is not a vague, hazy notion; it is quite ready, in every detail. The only effort I ask of you is not to say no.' As soon as I'm back in Paris, I'll get in touch with those leaders of war veterans whom I know. Besides, you say that some of them have already been felt out by their German comrades who wrote to them. That's fine. . . . Try on your side to let me have as quickly as possible the names of the leaders of veterans here who would be delegated to the commission. That way I can lay down a complete list. . . . The creators of complications won't know where to take hold."

Abetz had answered:

"Here, things will be settled very quickly. I'm coming to Paris myself in a few days. I'll see you immediately. I think Herr von Ribbentrop will be coming to Paris, too. It's also possible that Oberlindober, the leader of the Front of War Veterans and head of all their organizations, who would naturally be our first delegate to the plebiscite commission, will make the trip. He can exchange views on practical details with his French comrades. . . . I'll take the liberty of bringing Herr von Ribbentrop to see you. You have no objection?"

"Certainly not; on the contrary, I'd be very happy to talk at length with him."

"And if need be, you might facilitate a personal contact between him and the French government—between him and M. Laval, for example—to whom you could have explained beforehand Herr von Ribbentrop's position here . . . his importance at present, and more especially for the future?"

"I'll see to it if necessary. . . . It won't be wasted

effort in any case for me to insist back there on the real part played by Herr von Ribbentrop. For the Quai d'Orsay is always inclined to be wary of people who don't appear in a perfectly clear official capacity . . . and I'm afraid they're not well up on just what's happening, either inside your regime or behind the scenes in your politics."

As soon as I was back in Paris, I attended to the Saar business. I went to the Quai d'Orsay. I saw Léger and Laval. I spoke to them about my stay in Berlin, taking care not to emphasize the exceptional nature of the reception given me, for without fail they'd have said: "Naturally! The Germans turned his head with their flowers and their fanfare! He couldn't see through their game." On the contrary, I presented the case with cold objectivity. Léger showed gentle obstinacy beneath his extreme courtesy. His opinion hadn't changed, either on the odds in the plebiscite or on the folly it would be for us to spare Nazi pride that test. He quoted the opinion of some foreign journalist or other, back from the Saar, who predicted a large minority of objectors, if not a majority.

"All right!" I exclaimed. "That's no longer the question. . . ." And I put before him the plan for a mixed commission of war veterans. I had had time by then to get into contact with the leaders of the principal

French groups, Henri Pichot among them. Their approval had been secured.

"We must be very careful," retorted Léger. "To place such responsibility in the hands of well-meaning but unprepared people is terribly risky. . . . It may be courting the very difficulties you imagine you'll avoid, which the Germans chose to scare you with."

Indeed, I felt that in his eyes the proposal had at least three invalidating defects: it came from the Germans; it tended to dispossess vested authority; last, and probably not the least of the grievances, it was transmitted by a completely unofficial person.

I tried to explain that I didn't trust Germany's intentions unconditionally any more than he did, but that, in my opinion, we must "play up" to her; that we had often already "played her down"; that it was "playing up" to jump at the proposals of an adversary when they happened to be reasonable; that, in a word, blind suspicion was as serious a cause of weakness as blind trust. Léger met all this with the impenetrable wisdom of the Quai d'Orsay.

The interview with Laval was less disappointing. It's true he avoided any statement on the plan itself, while admitting it was most interesting, and he thanked me for my collaboration in furthering better relations between France and Germany. He promised that the question would be most carefully examined. And then he went off into a sort of confession, made

198

in a very calm, rather cordial voice, with a note of good-natured familiarity (in which I could sense a kind of desire to echo some of Briand's inflexions).

"You see," he said, "I'm still young for a politician. Even at my age I've had almost all the personal satisfactions I could wish. My thirst for power and honours truly demands nothing more. So now I'd really like to work with no ulterior motive towards ends I believe in. And there's none I believe in more than peace. At heart, I've remained a Socialist. . . . I've kept my devotion to Briand. . . . The work of that man should be carried on . . . nothing discouraged him . . . he was infinitely subtle . . . but at the end of his life he put all his subtlety into serving peace. . . . I intend to keep the portfolio of Foreign Affairs as long as possible. I won't be tempted by anything else—if necessary, I'll sacrifice something to keep it—because I'm convinced nothing useful can be done in this place unless one stays a long time."

He spoke to me of the value he placed, in international negotiations, on direct conversations and man-to-man contacts. And I, who had just had an experience of that kind with the Nazi leaders, and had certainly not come back with the impression it had been useless, could only agree with him.

Then he spoke of his daughter, who worked with him constantly, and whose youthful ardour was cheering to him. And it was all very human and pleasant.

All these impressions were fresh in my mind when I got a call from Abetz:

"I'm in Paris . . . with Herr von Ribbentrop. . . . Could you receive us?"

"Certainly."

At that time I lived in a small apartment in the Hotel Pierre Ier. During that year of 1934, with so much political stir around me, the small apartment had received the most unexpected visitors and been the scene of interviews of singular interest. When necessary, the hotel doorman, a very discerning and trustworthy man, surrounded my visitors with a vigilance directed against intrusions, and even saw to it that as far as possible the rooms next to my apartment were rented only to perfectly innocent-looking strangers, who couldn't be suspected of being in the service of any kind of police, or even of some newspaper (to old ladies, for instance, foreign, and a little deaf, who didn't understand much French). You can imagine the precautions he lavished on Ribbentrop's visit, or rather visits, for there were two, which I returned at the Bristol Hotel, where he was staying. We met four times all together during that period.

Into my little blue drawing-room—pure 1925 in style—came a fairly tall, slender, spirited man, with amused eyes and thin, ironical lips, well dressed but without studied elegance, who spoke very good French in a clear voice, with a marked accent of the "distinguished" kind. He liked to move around; he'd get up, sit in another chair, light cigarettes. His conversation was animated, with quick shifts from one idea to another. He certainly attached great importance to the Saar affair. But he hardly mentioned it in our first interview. Even later on, Ribbentrop pretended to treat it as a problem which was no longer worth our lengthy discussion. "We agree, don't we, you and I?" he seemed to say; "so let the underlings muddle through now!"

Besides, had the idea for a commission of war veterans come from Ribbentrop himself? It was hardly probable; for Goebbels, and especially Rosenberg, wouldn't have spoken to me about it so enthusiastically. At present I'm rather inclined to think that the idea came from Abetz, but that while suggesting it to Ribbentrop, he had been clever enough to try it out like a pilot balloon in the Rosenberg sphere, so that both sides had the flattering feeling that it had originated with them. And Goebbels had done his usual job by shouting it through his megaphone.

The fact remains that if Ribbentrop had taken the trip to Paris this time, it was in the hope that his presence would be linked to a success. But he wished it to be quite clear that he played a more prominent part, and that his views went much further.

He spoke casually of the situation in general. He described himself as a good European first and foremost; and in his eyes the axis of Europe could only be situated in the west. A Franco-German misunderstanding which dragged on and grew worse was the height of absurdity. If that factor was not eliminated promptly, no lasting order could be established in Europe and that unfortunate continent would go headlong to final disintegration.

We alluded to that element, sentimental or passionate, which so often turns up complicating such problems, and to all the national prejudices which it keeps alive and embitters, making them into "hereditary hatreds". On Ribbentrop's face, at times the face of a witty, eighteenth-century sceptic, hovered a smile of ironic superiority.

"I'm in a fairly good position to know what hereditary hatreds are worth," he said, "and how seriously one should take them. Among my first childhood memories are certain of my grandfather's precepts. My people are from Hanover, and my grandfather was a staunch Hanoverian. He'd say again and again: 'Remember this, son, the Prussians are our enemies; they always have been, they always will be. . . . Have nothing to do with them.' "

Under his words a current of thoughts like these ran from him to me: "There are many fools in the world . . . they take a lot of room and at times make a lot of noise. . . . It sometimes happens by chance that they control powerful resources and so are able to do appalling damage. . . . It's up to people of our kind to watch out, isn't it? . . . and to prevent stupid mistakes."

The atmosphere in my small blue drawing-room was most pleasant. The man before me was clearly not one of those generous-hearted men, with a great soul, in whom a driving love for humanity exists, and an apostolic faith in the power of the spirit on this earth, the men I prefer above all others, through whom the divine impulse of the Ninth Symphony and of Hugo's poems finds recurring expression. But when such men are not available, I rather like to meet a different type, those continually silhouetted in the correspondence of Voltaire, Diderot, Grimm, or the memoirs of Casanova—men who are too subtle, too sceptical, and also too elegant, to have either partiality for the undertakings of imbeciles, madmen, and bloodthirsty rabble, or any wish to encourage them.

I thought, moreover: in the present state of affairs in Germany, only a man of this kind has any chance of counteracting the raving or ecstatic madmen who hold the helm. A man of profound faith, acting on the same plane as theirs, could only hurl himself against them desperately, and be broken. It's all to the good when, in his own small corner, there's an Abetz with that profound faith. He'll serve always as a hidden leaven. But it's a good thing to find above, in the sphere of visible power, a Talleyrand or a Metternich

—in other words, a true son of the eighteenth century, who adeptly manages to prevent lunatics from smashing things up.

So I worked all the more willingly to make the Saar affair go smoothly, as I believed anyway it was not to France's interest to be cantankerous over it.

Since I felt that the Quai d'Orsay was getting ready to bury the proposal, and that M. Laval, while granting the interview with Ribbentrop as requested and receiving him cordially, would allow himself to be manœuvred by his administration, I did not hesitate to swing around, attacking the government from the rear through public opinion. Till then the negotiation had remained confidential. I had the July 9th committee organize rapidly a large meeting at the Sorbonne. I made a long speech in which I explained the whole business, emphasizing what consequences it might have and how foolish it would be of France to reject a proposal so sensible and dextrous. Several speakers, belonging to the most diverse groups—socialist, radical, centre, right, heads of leagues—gave me their complete support. The audience, representing all the Parisian élite that counts, reacted in a way that could leave no trace of doubt in the observers sent by the government.

A few days later an official bulletin announced that France had just put before the League of Nations a new procedure for the Saar plebiscite. She asked to be released from supervising the plebiscite. The French troops would be replaced by an international contingent, supplied preferably by a certain number of countries quite neutral in the matter: Swedes, Dutch, and so forth.

The solution, which was not bad on the whole, and which was actually used, bore the unmistakable stamp of the Quai d'Orsay. It gave us partial satisfaction. It disarmed public opinion. It couldn't be considered disobliging by the Germans, and, if need be, Ribbentrop back in Berlin could boast that he had obtained appreciable concessions from a suspicious partner. But as a whole it had almost none of the psychological and moral advantages I found in the original plan.

About that time I had to discuss with the Germans two affairs which had no connection with politics or with the Saar question, but which I relate here just the same, as they throw an amusing light on certain aspects of Nazi mentality.

The first has to do with my story, *Donogoo*, which the powerful moving-picture corporation UFA had planned to film. We had agreed on essentials and the work of preparation had begun. But the cinema, like everything else, had to submit to vigilant censorship. Studying my text closely, a censor thought he detected a harsh caricature of the regime. Abetz got wind of this and took pains to prove to the aforesaid censor that the caricature couldn't be very accurate, nor could it spring from malicious intent on my part, since the tale had been written in 1919 and I'd have needed a supernatural gift of prophecy to foresee as early as that the peculiarities of the Third Reich. But the censor's religion was not an enlightened one, and it took Goebbels's personal intervention before the UFA was allowed to proceed with its work. At that time the Third Reich was still flirting with foreign literature, disclaiming any fear of it.

The other affair took place a little later and concerns *Men of Good Will*. One day in Paris one of Goebbels's emissaries called on me, to say:

"We intend to publish a translation of *Men of Good Will* in Germany."

"Fine," I answered.

"We wish the translation to be excellent. We don't want to repeat, with your work, the mistake made with the first translation of Proust."

"I couldn't ask more."

"At the moment in Germany there's only one man who seems to us able to do that translation properly."

"Ah!" I said with interest.

"The author of the second Proust translation."

"Seems to me an excellent recommendation."

"Unfortunately, he's a Jew. . . ."

"But so far as I'm concerned, that's no drawback. . . ."

"Yes, but for us it's a great nuisance. . . . So this is what we ask of you. Would you be kind enough to write a letter to Dr. Goebbels, stating your opinion that at the moment in Germany one man only is capable of translating your *Men of Good Will*, and that man is Herr Franz Hessel? . . . Dr. Goebbels, out of courtesy to you, will give the necessary orders, and the publisher will be authorized to have *Men of Good Will* translated by Herr Franz Hessel." That is what, indeed, took place.

Two years later, great changes had occurred. I was in London, where Ribbentrop was Ambassador. I made no move to see him. All I knew about his recent activity, all I heard in London, was of a kind to make me wish not to meet him. If his personality had evolved in this way, what sense was there in our having an interview? To all appearances he was now the brutal henchman and not the subtle moderator of the regime. In the accounts given me I saw no longer the pupil of Talleyrand or of Metternich, but some head of the Russian police under the Czars, whose scepticism, being of the coarsest kind, acted only to strengthen cynicism and callousness, or to mask in his own eyes the nature of his activities. I don't know whether Ribbentrop had tried to play the disdainful aristocrat in London, but he hadn't succeeded. The English considered him ill-mannered; and some of the

methods he was credited with using, to advance in
London society or to secure some influence there, had
classed him in English opinion as being far from a
great gentleman. As for the good European, dedicated to the reconstruction of the West, you were
laughed at if you asked what had become of him. Obviously, he was just an out-and-out wire-puller and
maker of intrigues, a gambler who would as soon bet
at one table as another, with absolute indifference to
the moral or even human value of means or ends.

In the days immediately before Munich, I had another occasion to wonder about the man and to spread
before me, like a hand of cards, the various mental
pictures I had of him. He had then fulfilled his supreme ambition, the one Abetz had told me in the
past it was our duty to further. He was the Reich's
Minister of Foreign Affairs. I first saw the dispatch,
then heard the oral report in which François-Poncet
gave an account of his interview with Hitler on the
morning of Wednesday, September 28, 1938. One detail struck me. François-Poncet stressed the fact that
while he was talking in the foreground with Hitler, in
his most moving tone, Ribbentrop sat in the background at a small table. And sometimes François-
Poncet found arguments or inflexions that affected
Hitler; for instance, by picturing the appalling risk an
aggression against Czechoslovakia might entail for
Germany herself. He could see the Chancellor's ex-

pression change, he began to weaken. Then a dry, mocking voice would be heard, and from his little table Ribbentrop would declare with an implacable and malevolent sneer:

"Certainly not, Your Excellency. We've foreseen everything. . . . We're adequately prepared for anything. . . ."

Then Hitler stiffened, hardened.

After Munich I saw Ribbentrop twice, at a dinner of the Ministry of Foreign Affairs, and at a dinner he himself gave at the German Embassy. It was at the time that the so-called Paris Pact was signed. We exchanged only a few remarks. He wanted to make me feel, by a word and a smile, that he remembered our past conversations very well. He even seemed to imply: "You see! We can be pleased, both of us. There were many detours, and some accidents on the way. But we're on the right road at last."

As for Abetz, I saw him also on those two occasions, but we spoke at much greater length. Since the beginning of 1935 I had met him two or three times at most, and in circumstances where we should have found it difficult to talk with any privacy. He might have asked to see me at home; but he hadn't tried to, for he was shrewd and knew perfectly well that I'd ask distressing questions about the course taken by Germany's politics, about the assaults on the peace of Europe and the independence of her neighbours, or those abominations which she was committing, with a persistence that excluded all hope of improvement, against her leading minds, against the Jews, against religious and moral liberties of all kinds. He also knew that, while missing no occasion of condemning Germany's conduct publicly and denouncing the peril to which the Nazi-Fascist contagion had exposed the world, I never ceased to use my influence with the French government, and occasionally other governments, along the lines which I had always followed: do the impossible to preserve peace; leave no pretext or excuse open to your foe for the day when he might want, at all costs, to unleash catastrophe. So I wasn't the one to be lectured on the subject; and even if, in 1936 or 1937, Abetz had been inclined to say to me with a reproachful air: "What a pity you're no longer working with as much ardour as before in the cause of Franco-German understanding! . . . You look a little disheartened . . ." he could hear my answer beforehand: "Are you laughing at me, Abetz my friend? Do you think I'm a fool? . . . I'd like to see the Nazi-Fascist plague wiped out one day without bloodshed. And you'll always find me ready to support anything which will lessen or avert the danger of war. . . . But don't ask me to trust the men in your regime . . . or even those who serve it with a somewhat too unshakable constancy."

On the evening in question, he was more explicit

and expansive than his chief. He had become an elegant diplomat in a well-tailored suit. He manifested great pleasure at seeing me again, and insisted on introducing to me the other members of the German delegation, including the jurist Schmidt (who was on the Armistice commission in June 1940). These gentlemen spoke with enthusiasm of my newly published *Verdun*. "The German translation must come out as soon as possible," they said. They took the opportunity to ridicule staff officers and generals in every country. Abetz, drawing me aside, declared: "I'm pleased. . . . You are, too, aren't you? . . . We've worked so hard to make this possible some day! Oh, I know—the circumstances aren't what we had dreamed. . . ." He added: "It's stupid to think that it's Italy who's our ally!" Two of his companions who heard the remark echoed his sentiments.

A month later, as I related in my third chapter, I sent the King's Man to Abetz . . . but with no result. Seven more months passed, and Ribbentrop went to sign the pact with Molotov, making war inevitable, condemning the West to catastrophe and Europe to chaos. Add another eleven months; and the papers we read on our way to exile told us Abetz was appointed German Ambassador to Paris—a Paris where German troops had been quartered for some weeks—and High Commissary for occupied France.

I thought I would make some comments upon the Nazi mystery. . . . As I reread the pages I have just written, I wonder whether it's worth while. Don't the facts and personalities speak clearly enough?

Did I deal, consistently, with criminals and traitors? Ah, no! It's more subtle than that. The men I dealt with were on the whole not worse than average; one might be clearly superior in moral quality, another clearly inferior; but they were all caught, enveloped, carried away by a system, stronger than they were, in which the very means of existence, the fundamental impulse, was crime and treachery. Ribbentrop, from the start, was certainly a cynic. But at another time, in another system, he would have found it good to work, in an urbane way, to establish European harmony and the supremacy of a reasonable West in which chosen minds would set the tone. Abetz was almost certainly a man of good will. I can't believe they lied to me, he and his wife, when they were in their poor lodging, with their little boy beside them.

Ribbentrop must have made the adjustment with no great heart-break. The problem for him was the making of his career. Abetz must have suffered certain pangs of anguish . . . at least I hope so. There are some feats which are beyond one. To remain a man of good will within such a system was like trying to keep a vow of chastity in a brothel.

We who were outside the system sinned too often, if

not out of readiness to oblige, at least out of leniency and a sort of lazy optimism. We didn't wish to acknowledge as impossible the good fortune the future might hold for us, the wonderful fading-out of that nightmare.

Many mistakes made from the outside were excusable, and they involved a wager on the future which was not so very absurd. It would have seemed inspired if the future had borne it out. But at one definite moment an absolutely inexcusable error was committed, for which France, Europe, the world, are now paying the price. And it's the story of that error, and what underlies it, that still remains for me to tell you in my last chapter.

VII

WHO SAVED FASCISM?

You HAVE noticed perhaps that in this book I have refrained from using high-flown language about the present situation. But don't think, because of that, that I'm less aware than others of the gravity, the horror even, of the situation, or that I attempt to reduce it to the ordinary historical scale. On the contrary, the more I think over the catastrophe we are living through, the more persuaded I am that it goes beyond any our fathers have known since the end of the Middle Ages. It is truly a catastrophe of the first magnitude. Our contemporaries, far from exaggerating its importance, are even inclined in my opinion to take it much too easily for granted, as long as a certain distance still separates them from its principal focus, and to believe a miracle will preserve them—the miracle which has steadily been denied up to now to those who nursed the same cowardly hope. The exact extent of the disaster will only be measured later by historians—if any historians are left—and it is probable that they will express themselves as appraisers sometimes do after investigating a fire: "The losses are unfortunately greater than first estimates had led us to suppose."

In any case, what can be asserted even now—that is, at a time when vast developments of the scourge must still be anticipated—is that the disaster has already amply justified the fears of those who for the last twenty years doggedly repeated that a new war of nations was the greatest conceivable misfortune, and who had put all their energy, all their ingenuity, into preventing it. Let us even say boldly that these men in what they feared had underestimated what reality held in store for us. For, in general, they had not envisaged a victory, even temporary, for the evil principle. They had not imagined a Europe like the one under our eyes, entirely delivered up to the triumphant fury of Hitlerism, and around that Europe a demoralized world, where most people are half frozen with terror and where a few others secretly itch to be accomplices, or openly bargain for their complicity.

Be that as it may, we must pay homage to those men—even if we are to have no witness to that homage but eternal Justice. All our judgments on the years preceding the war, on the nations and their politics, on any one of the individuals who here or there had a public part to play, must be dominated by the following question: "Did they wish to avoid this war, and did they hate it beforehand? Were their efforts, whether fortunate or unfortunate, directed against this war?"

In this connection it is impossible to denounce with too much vigour a sophism which is spreading now, with the result that it is poisoning what is left of public conscience throughout the world. The sophism consists in a scandalous confusion about the word "responsibility." We hear, for instance: "Chamberlain, Halifax, Daladier, and so on are responsible for what happened . . ." or "England is responsible . . ." or else "Roosevelt, for his part, is responsible . . ." and the same word is used when speaking of Hitler, Mussolini, Göring, Nazi Germany, Fascist Italy. . . . How can people fail to see that there is no relation between the two orders of facts, and that to use the same word in the two cases without clearly stressing the profound change of meaning is to perform a sleight-of-hand benefiting only the enemies of mankind, and to discourage beforehand all people of good will. What is the use of giving oneself endless trouble for years to ward off the world's principal scourge, only to be bracketed one day with the very makers of the scourge!

Yes, we can blame Chamberlain, Daladier, others. . . . Yes, we can blame England. . . . Yes, we can blame all those whose efforts towards peace turned out badly. The aim of this book has been precisely to bring home to people, in some familiar and personal way, how attempts made with deep sincerity in the service of the noblest of causes can be foiled by events or thwarted in the end by lack of tenacity or vigilance. It also shows that in a world which has reached a tragic phase, the will to good is no longer enough, it may even become a cause of weakness when confronted by the will to evil. But, in heaven's name, don't let us lose sight of the fact that in one case the whole fault was lack of suspicion, of hardness, or of promptness in answering threat by threat, violence by violence; while in the other case, the crime in question was positive, deliberate, long premeditated. Between the responsibility of the former and the responsibility of the latter lies the entire abyss of human morality. Has anyone ever thought of putting on an equal footing the mistake of the good man who sleeps in his apartment at night behind an inadequately bolted door, and the crime of gangsters who, after having broken in the door with the latest thing in tools, end by assassinating the good man in his bed? If the day ever came when public conscience admitted with a shrug a certain equivalence in those two responsibilities, then on that day humanity would

217

have returned definitely to the laws of the primeval forest.

It is, in fact, one of the sad things of the present time to see the men who struggled to preserve the peace of the world, each according to his means and the conception he had formed of risks and possibilities, now forget their guild of yesterday, in panicky terror of "responsibilities". For instance, I read the other day that Georges Bonnet, about whom I have given favourable testimony, was corroborating vehemently Daladier's accusers on the question of precipitating war. If the news is accurate, it is not to Bonnet's honour. He knows perfectly well that all he could have done in September 1939 was to delay war for six months. He can answer that such a delay was not to be sneered at; and he would be right, on principle. But Daladier can retort, what is truer still, that there was no way of holding the nation for another six months in the state of military mobilization and psychological tension in which it was, or of throwing it back into such a state six months later after a false lull. Therefore to give in once more in 1939 was to deliver up to Hitler in 1940 France and Europe, tied hand and foot.

We must beware of everything that bears any resemblance to these distracted accusations and exonerations. "Was that man at the bottom of his heart for peace, or for war? Did he work in the naked truth of

conscience to maintain peace, or to unleash war?"—
that is once again the great question, the only question, I would say to believers, of concern to God. We
must bear it in mind even when we approach what I
call the border-line cases. I mean by that the cases in
which we need great self-control not to hurl sweeping
condemnations, whether it be—as with Gamelin—that
the man's profession makes ludicrous any excuse he
might seek in his love of peace (for a determined
pacifist is absolutely not obliged to become generalissimo); or—as with Leopold III—that a final act, of
classic gravity and of a kind to stir popular emotion
—like the betrayal of his allies in full battle—should
confound indulgence and throw suspicion on all
former behaviour.

But my readers must have noticed that I didn't even
refuse to discover signs of good will at one time in an
Abetz, if not in a Ribbentrop. And why not? We must
expect such discoveries rather, when we abandon a
melodramatic view of the world. It's highly improbable that all the good should be on one side and all
the evil on the other. But granted that, one must acknowledge all the more vigorously that certain "sys-
tems" are radically detestable, since their incontro-
vertible effect is to make raving madmen out of simple
megalomaniacs whom another system would have
rendered harmless, and henchmen of evil out of men
who by nature perhaps tended towards good will.

That is the truth which we must not allow any sophism or hypocritical indulgence to invalidate. When Fascism, and Nazism in its wake, established themselves in Europe, they implanted a destructive principle (the cost of which rendered worthless the few improvements they might bring—for instance, in governmental efficiency, output of collective work, or cure for political haggling). That destructive principle was the rehabilitation of violence both in individual and in national relationships, and principally of war; a rehabilitation one might have thought impossible after the 1914–18 ordeal, and after three centuries at least of mankind's groping march towards a universal morality.

That destructive principle, once inoculated into the organism of a civilization, tended to develop according to a fatal process of which biology offers us a model: neither cancer nor a bacterial invasion spontaneously recedes; they must be opposed, according to the type of resistance, by counter-attacks or by surgical interventions. Ideologies and regimes which, far from condemning war, exalted its principle— which proclaimed, for instance, in the words of that imbecile Marinetti—the man d'Annunzio called *il cretino fosforescente*—"war, the only hygiene of nations"—could only culminate in war, dragging the world with them if they were allowed to follow their bent. And indeed there was reason for men of good will, consecrated to peace, to draw back when confronted with a bloody preventive operation which made a mockery of their faith. But when history's unforeseen movement, a concurrence of events one might call providential, brought a chance to get rid of that destructive principle at one blow, and probably without shedding a drop of blood, you would think, wouldn't you, that these men would have jumped at the chance, grasped it with enthusiasm, held on to it with energy? And if they failed to do that, especially if they decided not to do it in spite of a clear conception of the opportunity and of what was at stake, is it not true that then their negative responsibility went far beyond the ones considered above? And if, not content with letting the destructive principle slip out of their grasp—as a policeman might let go a gangster he had just arrested—they acted as if they were "in cahoots" with him and winked knowingly at him while they held him, letting him race off, his fury increased by humiliation and rancour, does not their responsibility in this stop being negative? Does it not become comparable with that of the criminal they deliberately saved? Doesn't the blood of the future victims, the horror of the coming destructions, fall almost equally on the heads of the accomplice and the criminal?

All my life I shall remember that afternoon of

October 3, 1935. The sun shone brightly. I was strolling along the boulevard des Italiens—to be exact, on the sidewalk between the rue Favart and the rue de Richelieu, near the restaurant Poccardi. Newsboys were everywhere, with stacks of papers. The big headlines read: "Adowa Bombed by Italian Air Force."

I felt as if the visible world was brutally rent apart. The early autumn sun was still as lovely and as mild. But it was now one of those falsely smiling suns which shine on human disasters with particular cruelty. For it was disaster we were facing. I was sure of that. An old image of Roman mythology was coming to life again: I thought I could hear in the distance the doors of the Temple of Janus, closed during sixteen years, turn on their hinges with a sinister sound. Now that they were open, all that was worst became possible, and all the effort expended on what was better was in vain. At the cost of millions of dead in 1914–18, at the cost of all the suffering accumulated and handed down by the World War, and all sorts of racking meditations, humanity had reached a result of extraordinary moral import: war had been declared *taboo*. Oh, of course, as always happens with moral prohibitions, some people could cheat on the new taboo; others even openly jeered at it with scandalous infractions. But it stood its ground, and there was no absurdity in the belief that time would increase its strength; that the further we got from the period of its origin, the

222

greater the mystical respect nations would feel towards it. The Italian bombs had sent it flying to pieces.

You may say that before the bombs Fascist vociferations had already scoffed at the taboo and glorified war. True; and we must now admit that this crime in spirit wholly contained the later crime in fact. But it was permissible before the Adowa bombs to take such declamations as purely bellicose trumpetings, designed to bolster up a naturally unmartial people. The bombs dissipated all ambiguity.

You may also say that even earlier there had been very serious violations of the taboo: like Japan's attempt against China at the end of 1931, or the Chaco war in South America. But, rightly or wrongly, those unfortunate events had not been charged with such decisive and symbolic importance. First, geographically these conflicts were very far from the inflammatory centre of the world which Europe remained. Then, the respective opponents did not seem inclined, from what motives it is difficult to judge, to make a real world affair of their quarrel. China, specifically, when attacked, had seemed to claim the intervention of the League of Nations only rather softly. Japan on her side had managed to give her aggression the character of gradual intervention in favour of a young state aspiring to independence. These excuses were obviously trumped up, and we must now admit that the League committed a grave fault against its ideal and its purpose by failing to take any decisive initiative. But it is by trumped-up excuses that taboos have often been preserved; and common wisdom could maintain it was not to the League's interest to bring its authority into dangerous action except in cases where it was formally and solemnly compelled to act.

With the Adowa bombs, there was no way of stopping one's ears or of simulating absent-mindedness. Everything had piled up to give the affair its maximum moral repercussion. After long weeks of diplomatic conversations, in which an attempt was made to persuade Italy not to aggravate matters, to be satisfied with very substantial concessions at Ethiopia's expense, to abandon her ostentatious preparations for aggression, the League of Nations was appealed to; the procedure had got under way with all dispatch. Committees were formed, *of the Thirteen,* and *of the Five,* to study the question thoroughly and search for a compromise acceptable to both parties while sparing the Italian government the humiliation of having to bow before a condemnation. At the same time both parties, which meant Italy, were solemnly enjoined to commit no act that might break or even disturb the state of peace as long as the case was pending before the court of nations. The Adowa bombs savagely challenged this procedure—it was almost as if, in a court itself, one of the litigants drew a revolver and fired at his adversary under the noses of the judges. As a crowning mockery, it was Italy herself who had requested earlier that Ethiopia be admitted to the League of Nations, guaranteeing the worthiness of her candidate.

But in the moral skies of the time there existed a quite extraordinary atmospheric condition which amplified the resonance of the affair. I have already alluded to it in my chapter on England. Eminent representatives of the intellectual and moral élite of Great Britain, under the impulse and high leadership of Lord Robert Cecil, organized an immense poll of opinion on the essential problems of peace. Increasingly widespread collaboration was volunteered from the public at large, schools, churches, and various associations, to stimulate and collect the votes. More than eleven million voices had spoken, which was unprecedented on the face of this earth as a spontaneous manifestation of opinion; that is to say, in what was neither a plebiscite nor a referendum ordered by public authority. And those eleven million voices, which could be said to represent everything Great Britain possessed of conscience and of mind, demanded in effect a strengthening of the League of Nations, obligations imposed on its members, material means put at its disposal to curb and punish aggression against peace. That admirable movement, called the *Peace Ballot,* which will for ever stand to England's honour, had its roots deep in moral conscience. It was inspired by men who meditate and study, not by politicians; it was nourished with enthusiasm and was as uncalculating as the Declaration of the Rights of Man and of the Citizen in France in 1789. It was destined to radiate swiftly, to create a precedent, a new date of birth in the history of humanity. In France almost immediately there was talk of organizing a similar ballot. But, as I have said, on its way the movement happened to encounter as a decisive test the Ethiopian question. Never before had an affair between nations had so many chances not to pass unnoticed or be abandoned to specialists in chancelleries; and so many chances of becoming a dramatic issue for universal conscience, and an opportunity for the supporters of good throughout the world to estimate their numbers.

In the balance hung not only the interests of a particular nation, more or less to be pitied, but the very conception of Law, International Justice, and the respect due a nation as such, whatever its special merits. If Law and Justice were flouted in such a striking case, and with impunity, the defeat was beyond remedy, and the supporters of evil—that is, of return to the age of violence and darkness—could raise their heads and leer. The Ethiopian case, in short, had every element necessary to make it a Dreyfus case on the international level.

A week later I was on my way to Geneva. I was going to attend the Assembly of the League of Nations, which had been called into extraordinary session following the Italian aggression. Many people were wondering whether the League would show itself equal to the occasion, or take refuge in formalities and fine words. This could be for the League either a triumphant resurrection or a collapse. I also wished to make contact with some of the men heading the League, with the specific purpose of assuring them that the moral élite of France did not share the attitude of part of the Parisian press, notoriously in the pay of the Fascist government. I knew I'd see Langevin there (the world-renowned scientist).

The preceding days in Paris had been days of steadily rising agitation. A certain number of writers and journalists, more or less openly Fascist, retrograde academicians, future fifth-column members or plain hirelings—those who now are licking the boots of Hitler's generals—had been brazen enough to publish a manifesto which, in the name of Latin fraternity and the spirit of the West (!), showered indignation on those among us who, in England and France, condemned the Italian aggression and demanded vigorous international sanctions in this instance. We had immediately answered their insolent text. I had drawn up the counter-manifesto, with the help of Louis Aragon and Luc Durtain, around midnight in a small café on the rue des Martyrs, the very night when *Le Temps* published the declaration of the future fifth column. True, I felt somewhat distrustful of Aragon, because of his Communist connections and his genius for intrigue. But he happened at the time to be serving the good cause, putting his ardour to all sorts of practical uses. Our manifesto immediately collected numerous and important signatures—but there were some curious abstentions, Georges Duhamel's, for example, which Luc Durtain failed to get in spite of all his efforts. (Duhamel at the time was preparing his candidacy for the Academy. Such is the obnoxious influence of that institution I've so carefully kept clear of. . . . I think Duhamel must feel rather sorry about it, and must have realized that the Adowa bombs had a numerous offspring.)

As I drove along the road to Geneva, I was thinking of a luncheon which, unless I'm mistaken, took place in the second half of February 1935, the memory of which had recently gained significance for me (in the interval it had entirely slipped my mind). It was a private luncheon at the home of friends, and I sat almost opposite Pierre Laval. We had of course spoken a great deal about foreign politics. He was just back from Rome, where he had seen the Pope and Mussolini.

"Well," Laval had said, in his easy-going way and rather slow voice with its trace of peasant accent, "I soon felt at ease with them. . . . It was very simple. I just fell back on my past. . . . When I faced the Pope, I remembered our village priest long ago, when I was a child. I pretended we were there together, he grown very old now, and I no longer—quite certainly no longer—a child. So our interview went very well. . . . With Mussolini, I recalled my youth as a Socialist. . . . He recalled his too. . . . That immediately created a common ground between us, something dear to us both. . . . We began with an understanding—instead of with a misunderstanding." A little later Laval, turning to me, had said with the studied offhandedness of a peasant, back from the tavern, who wards off reproaches by saying to his wife about a neighbour with whom the family has quarreled for a long time: "Of course, I gave him that measly little spring, you know, at the end of the field":

". . . Of course, I gave him Abyssinia. . . ."

He had added with his conciliatory smile, the smile of a man who doesn't dramatize:

". . . What would you have done in my place?"

In February I made no answer. I was merely surprised. I hadn't any notion that the Abyssinian ques-

229

tion (Abyssinia and Ethiopia, as you know, are two names for the same country) had suddenly come into prominence in the Rome interviews; and probably the Quai d'Orsay itself was unprepared. I knew that Laval had gone down there intending to "fix things up" and to give Mussolini a few "small presents". As a matter of fact, it's only the "small presents" that official communiqués had played up. How had the idea of a present the size of Abyssinia ever cropped up? Perhaps during one of those talks with no protocol, no agenda, those friendly talks which their common "Socialist background" (h'm!) had fostered between the two? I didn't even remember then, when listening to Laval, that Ethiopia was a member of the League of Nations. I didn't quite know either what Laval meant by "to give", but I presumed he hadn't acted rashly and hadn't "given" Abyssinia—which after all didn't belong to him—without among other precautions getting England's advice.

The remark (the scrupulous accuracy of which I guarantee, though it has little chance of appearing in M. Laval's memoirs) had come back to me when the affair began to take a bad turn; and when in August and September Laval protested at the top of his lungs to all those who in various quarters suspected him of rashness and imprudence: "Why, not at all! I made no such promise to M. Mussolini. . . . In the first place, I'd never take it upon myself to dispose of a country which in no way belongs to France!" "What nerve the man has," I had thought, as the words he pronounced in February rang in my ears with hallucinatory precision. "Well! He's trying to get out of a tight corner. . . . It won't be so easy!" And I said it to myself again on the road to Geneva.

The session of the Assembly was really of dramatic interest. The October 10th meeting in particular was of majestic dimension. It took place in the large hall of the Electoral Building. (The new Palace of the Ariana was not finished.)

Describing the meeting at the time, I compared it to the famous night of August 4 in the French Revolution. It deserved the comparison because of the emotion with which it was charged, the enthusiasm (not theatrical, but deep) with which it fired those present, and the lofty ideals at stake. Like the night of August 4th, it could become the dawn of an immense hope, the starting-point of a new era. This time it was not the privileged classes who came freely to offer up their privileges on the altar of their country. It was the nations—the blind and selfish nations whose stupidity had stained centuries with blood— who came to say in solemn words: "Henceforward something exists greater than ourselves: the Justice of the world; the common Law of the peoples. We bow before it of our own free will. And we agree that any one of us who violates this law shall be punished."

Yes, we saw that hour, great among the greatest hours of history. We saw the representatives of forty-two nations come up to the rostrum one after another, and each spoke for one minute, declaring in about the same words and, with certain exceptions, in the same language, French:

"We are friendly to Italy, and as a people we desire to be on good terms with her. But as Italy has violated the pact of the League of Nations in a completely unwarranted manner, we condemn her action and are ready to apply all the sanctions which may be voted."

Thereupon the speaker walked down the steps and went back to his place amid the religious silence of the Assembly. The next one got up and walked to the rostrum.

The repetition of gesture and formula increased the emotion. Its monotony gave it majesty. One felt that a rite was being created. It was in fact the first time the assize of humanity, the Amphictyonic Council of the modern world, functioned completely.

The lobbies of the Assembly were no less exceptional in aspect. There were no longer detached smiles, careless remarks, which in other circumstances were considered good form. Faces were grave, or exhilarated, or even enthusiastic. I met the soothsayers of the Quai d'Orsay: Léger, Massigli. They said:

"It's magnificent!" Their eyes were shining. From their lips came no reminder of the famous "Quai d'Orsay scepticism". They too believed we were witnessing the founding of a new order.

During a recess I accosted Laval in the entrance hall. He was alone with Léger at the time. I said to Laval without preamble:

"Well, *Monsieur le Président,* it's great! . . . And what a part France can play!"

His smile was embarrassed, evasive. It had a suggestion of "Let's not be carried away."

I went on bluntly:

"There's one thing we must put a stop to immediately, because it's not to France's honour." (People had spoken to me about it as soon as I got to Geneva, but I knew it all too well already.) ". . . A part of our press is sold to Italy—that's notorious—and is campaigning shamelessly. . . . You have ways of preventing such scandal. . . ."

Laval assumed an air of good-natured amusement:

"Oh, really? Sold to Italy? . . . Oh! Isn't that greatly exaggerated?"

Over Laval's shoulder Léger signed to me: "Go ahead! Come out with it!"

I did come out with it, and made it quite clear to Laval that he'd be wrong if he defended the venal press. He went on smiling, but he felt ill at ease. He took some incident or other in the conversation as a

233

pretext to say jokingly to Léger:

"Well, well! I feel almost like going back to Paris—h'm? . . . Jules Romains could take my place."

I met Eden, Politis, Motta (several times President of the Swiss Confederation), Bech, the Premier of Luxembourg, and many others. We had interviews of varying lengths. They had all been gripped by the same contagious faith. Eden seemed to me fired with ardour and determination. He thanked me for an article I had published a couple of days before in Paris, in which I had appealed to the French conscience, showing that the Geneva Assembly was about to tackle an immense task on which hung the future of civilization. The article had been widely read in Assembly circles and everybody mentioned it to me. It had been read with a sigh of relief, for the "venal press" had stirred up painful doubt about the attitude of France.

I saw Baron Aloisi, Italy's delegate to the Assembly, walk out. He was trying to smile, but his face was that of a man whose cause is lost and who avoids the eyes of others. As he was personally greatly liked, people were sorry that—by delegation—he had to carry the weight of universal reprobation. "In his heart of hearts, he thinks as we all do," one of his friends told me. "He's spent part of his day trying to telephone to Mussolini to beg him to listen to reason. But Mussolini, it appears, evades the calls."

After the session I went, accompanied by Langevin and Pierre Cot, to pay a visit to our friend Beneš, who was then President of the League of Nations. We reassured Beneš as to the real feelings of the French masses. "Yes, but Laval? . . ." he said. I had to admit that, an hour before, I hadn't been very favourably impressed by Laval. But, to balance that, the state of mind of the Quai d'Orsay seemed as satisfactory as possible.

"They'll keep him in line," I said. "And we'll have an eye on him too."

We spoke of the historical magnitude of the situation. President Beneš, in a tone of solemn conviction, said exactly these words:

"If we do our duty, peace will be preserved in the world for twenty years at least."

Then we philosophized about Mussolini and the fate in store for him.

"Fundamentally," Beneš remarked, "up to now he's always miscalculated in matters of foreign policy. . . . He's living on a false reputation in that respect."

We spoke of Hitler, who was lying low. Not a whisper came out of Berlin. The Nazis were trying to escape notice.

"They're kind of caught, too," we said. . . . "Today's meeting alone, which they can't keep entirely from public opinion, will make a deep impression in Germany. But if tomorrow proves that henceforward a policy of violence is impossible, there's nothing left for them but to shut up shop."

My friend Salvador de Madariaga—one of the most luminous minds of the Europe of yesterday—who had been chosen as president of the Committee of the Thirteen, and of the Five, and who therefore knew better than anyone else in the world the files on the Ethiopian affair, had been kind enough to invite me to dinner at the Hotel des Bergues and to give me the entire evening. There were four or five of us. Madariaga, too, was full of enthusiasm and confidence. In his perfect French—slightly tinged with a charming accent which might have been that of Bordeaux or Bayonne—he said as he shook my hand:

"Mussolini is through . . ." (and instantly generalizing on the proposition, as we all do in our minds, he added more familiarly than Beneš but with the same idea:) "if we just hang on, very soon the world will be rid of all those skunks. . . . Yes, old chap, we'll be able to get back to work and breathe again. . . ."

Then he came out with all sorts of anecdotes and precise details connected with the affair. We discussed Mussolini's psychology and what attitude he'd take in the following days and weeks.

"Now he can't back out of it," said Madariaga, "he's gone too far. . . . He'd fall immediately. . . . So he's got to go on with it—till the day it's no longer possible.

He'll find a more or less theatrical end for himself.
Some Italians here claim they already know how it'll
go: he'll take his plane and get lost out at sea. . . .
But others say the violent gang in the Fascist party,
those who have the greatest crimes on their con-
sciences and who know they can't save their necks,
will go to desperate lengths and put the peninsula to
fire and sword before they themselves go to the execution block. . . ."

Then Madariaga said, making fun of it (but in his
Spanish soul perhaps a trace of involuntary belief
mingled with the fun):

"You know that Mussolini's astrological theme—so
an astrologer explained to me the other day—is quite
similar to Napoleon's, though of course more mediocre in kind. Disaster is written in it, at about the
same age. And apparently death at sea is easily dis-
cernible. To die on St. Helena is a way of dying at
sea, isn't it? An airplane would only modernize the
theme."

These are the dreams of liberation on which the
world lived at Geneva through its representatives in
those memorable October days. And I rightly say the
world, for some American friends I met the next day
—Edgar Mowrer, for instance—had been uplifted just
as we were by our great hope. The famous slogan
(such a fine one, too, for it conveys everything) which
events too often had mocked: "Make the world safe

for democracy," was flying once again at the mast-head, saluted by the acclamations of free peoples.

The following 2nd of December, towards the end of the afternoon, I went to the Palais Bourbon to see Yvon Delbos, my old friend, who was then vice-president of the Chamber of Deputies. He received me in one of the pretty, newly decorated little rooms, called "offices of the vice-presidents". I forget what I had gone to talk about. He seemed absent-minded and yet stirred by some inner excitement, like a man whose heart was filled to overflowing with some very pleasant thing—like the secret of a new love, for instance—about which he refrained from talking.

As I got up to take my leave, he said:

"Can I give you a lift? . . . We'll chat a little longer. I'll drop you where you wish. . . ."

When we were in his car, he was silent for a moment; then leaning towards me:

"Listen," he said, "I think we'll be rid of Fascism in a fortnight . . . and of Nazism three weeks later. This time the trick is played!"

"What!" I exclaimed with a rush of joy. "What do you mean?"

Delbos was of all men the least inclined to talk big or to get wound up. A remark like this, coming from him, was certainly not a random shot. He leaned forward again:

"It's still a secret, of course; but I can let you in on it. . . . Herriot just told me a few minutes ago that this morning the government received an ultra-confidential appeal from Mussolini . . . and guess what the appeal was! I'll give you a thousand guesses. . . ."

"No—I'm completely in the dark. . . ."

"Well, Mussolini is asking us to apply the oil embargo to him immediately." He added with a laugh: "Without our saying, of course, that he asked us to. . . ."

"But why?"

"So that he can say to the Italian people: 'This time there's no way of resisting—they're strangling me. . . . I'm going.' "

"Then he is going?"

"Certainly. It's a question of days only. . . . Besides we have other indications. They're already concerned with the government which will have to replace him . . . and the disturbances which must be avoided."

We agreed that with Mussolini out of the way, the democratic wave of liberation would soon reach Germany. To be sure, a backwash was to be feared, and desperate ventures would have to be faced. But we'd pull through all that and with pleasure! January or February of the new year would bring to the world, which would hardly believe its eyes, the end of the great nightmare.

We separated on the rue de Rivoli, at the corner of the Palais du Louvre, both buoyed up by our glad secret. Never had the air of a December night seemed to me so light to breathe.

That was really because, since the glorious October days in Geneva, we had alternated between hope and anxiety. We were quick to feel that the machinery of the first sanctions had scarcely been set in motion when a great deal of underground activity was expended to reassure Mussolini on the one hand, and on the other to restrain the ardour of the English government, which set the pace. Actually the first sanctions voted by the Geneva Assembly, which affected only a certain number of commercial transactions and of war supplies, were in the mind of the League just a beginning. They were to become gradually more severe if, in the meantime, the aggressor did not give in. Two more serious penalties prescribed, and already under study, were the closing of the Suez Canal—which would cut the Italian army in East Africa from all supplies—and an embargo on importations of fuel into Italy, the effect of which would be no less decisive. No doubt an attempt at violent resistance by Italy could be expected. England had informed Geneva that she would eventually put her fleet at the disposition of the League of Nations; she had asked France at the same time to lend her, if need be, the naval bases of Toulon and

Bizerte. Naturally, the preliminary steps remained strictly confidential, and Samuel Hoare could still declare to the House of Commons on October 22 that England for the time being did not intend to close the Suez Canal or to go on to military sanctions. That was literally true; and one could still hope that the culprit would promptly show adequate repentance. Besides, even then England could see that the French government wasn't playing fair. An answer concerning the bases was avoided. They were not formally refused. But was there any reason to bother about them so soon, when military sanctions hadn't been considered yet officially? Which didn't prevent reassuring messages from slipping through surreptitiously to Rome: "Don't worry. We won't lend our naval bases for action against you."

In Great Britain itself, certain admirers of Mussolini and his regime undermined the government's work. Almost everywhere papers in the pay of Fascist propagandists spread the notion that it was naïve of nations to play England's game by applying sanctions which were very hard on their trade and by facing the risk of war against a marvellously well-armed Italy, wrought up to legitimate fury. England was only following her own selfish interests, trying to remain mistress of the route to India. And, as usual, she cloaked herself in virtuous pretexts, while trying to make others pay the bill. . . . As a result, the sanctions were half-heartedly applied by most countries, or even sabotaged.

But situations have a force of their own. The enthusiasm of October 10 was not easy to quench. In spite of everything, the first sanctions were having their effect. Behind its Fascist apparatus, real Italy was more anxious than whipped up. She knew perfectly well that Mussolini's rantings would break against the police of nations, and she was getting ready to abandon the leader who had brought upon her the reprobation of the entire world. Mussolini knew that too. He had just found this way out: "Show quite clearly you've got a stranglehold on me, so that I can shout at least that you're loathesome, that you're not playing fair, and that I'm quitting."

Alas! The fortnight set by Delbos went by; then the three weeks after that. In vain. January 1937 didn't bring the end of the nightmare for Europe and the world. Far from it! Mussolini gradually got his second wind, went on with the conquest of Abyssinia, and took on his old insolence; while his pal, Hitler, having just recovered from the terrible shock he'd got out of solidarity, was preparing to send his troops into the Rhineland. And both, as a revenge for their common anxiety, were beginning to contemplate the Spanish coup.

What had happened?

It's a question which I for one studied as closely as I could, turning to the most trustable sources.

Among these "sources" there are some I can't name. But I shall make no casual statements.

The first question to be settled is this: At the beginning of December 1935 was Mussolini—and consequently Fascism in Europe—really defeated, providing only that events had been allowed to take their course?

I answer outright: yes.

And I add: Fascism would have collapsed, not perhaps without some backwash and a little damage, but without war, without anything bearing resemblance to war: therefore practically without bloodshed.

I know the argument against it: England was in a dangerous state of disarmament. Her navy wasn't ready. Mussolini knew it. Before capitulating, he'd have staked everything on one throw without hesitation.

That's only retrospective bluff on the part of some, a poor excuse on the part of others.

True, the English navy wasn't at the height of its power. The naval reserve in particular hadn't been built up again. But can any of us be made to believe that Great Britain hadn't the means to dominate the

Mediterranean and all its issues, including the canal, especially, as should have been taken for granted, when backed by the French fleet and with our naval bases at her disposal? Experience in the present war leaves us no uncertainty in that respect. Mussolini knew that perfectly. If he had pretended not to, others in Italy knew it and would have prevented him from making that crucial blunder. (This has no connection, you understand, with the situation in May-June 1940. And even in May-June 1940 Mussolini had to overcome serious opposition.)

But one piece of evidence among others is conclusive. I got it in 1937 from His Excellency Yotaro Sugimura. Yotaro Sugimura was Japan's Ambassador to Rome in December 1935. I needn't stress the fact that when he spoke to me in 1937, as the Italo-Japanese flirtation was then at its warmest, he had every reason to treat Italy, her leader, and her regime with all due care. And yet to my question: "At the beginning of December 1935 did Mussolini really feel he was through?" he answered, weighing his words, but without hesitation: "Yes. It's not a hypothesis. It's a certainty. I saw Mussolini, with whom I was on good terms, quite often during those days. I can assert that he thought he was done for. He always kept a loaded revolver in his desk, within reach—he showed it to me. He was prepared to blow out his brains at any minute."

Other proofs exist. I must say they're delicate to present, for I'd have to name people who haven't the slightest desire to be named. (It's true one of them is dead.) We'll leave it at this: a substitute government was ready in Italy. In addition to important personalities in the regime, ones who had always tended to moderation and disapproved of the Ethiopian venture from the start—some of them held prominent posts abroad—it contained a few members of the old court parties and some émigrés. The English government had been sounded out and warned. It was entirely up to the French government to allow similar overtures. Perhaps it did allow them. Perhaps it betrayed them.

That brings us to the second question: Who saved Fascism? Naturally, the answer is not so simple.

First comes the case of M. Laval. All told, his is a primary responsibility. It goes right back to the origins of the affair. If he hadn't "given" Ethiopia to Mussolini, to use his own expression, Mussolini would certainly have thought twice before launching such a venture. But Mussolini was justified in saying to himself: "If they want to get in my way, France will keep out of it. I'll manage."

Such a deliberate paralysis of France never ceased to weigh on events.

But, at the beginning of December, International

Justice had carried the day, try as they would to make her advance halting.

What exactly was the shady game played between the 2nd and the 10th of December? December 10 is the day on which the Hoare-Laval compromise was made public. (The plan, against all expectations, offered Italy very substantial privileges in Ethiopia, equivalent in many respects to a protectorate.) Mr. Eden, who fought bravely for the good cause in that very period, but without great success, will certainly one day have the most interesting revelations to make on the subject. In the meantime, we must suppose that the desperate appeal made by Mussolini on December 2 was kept from the English government. (Actually, the existence of the appeal has never before to my knowledge been revealed.) It's probable, rather, that Laval immediately took steps to save his "pal" in Rome, and that it seemed to him a good way out to suggest to Samuel Hoare—who probably was no more conspicuous for his subtlety than the average British conservative—the plan for a compromise which put off further sanctions, completely overwhelmed the defenders of International Justice by its immorality, divided British opinion, and finally gave Mussolini a breathing-space, time to break the grip which had clamped down on him and to get back his self-assurance with the characteristic rapidity of adventurers.

But it would be unfair to let all the responsibility

weigh on M. Laval. The English carry their share; first, in a general and inveterate fashion through the lack of decision they've always shown, their perverse leaning towards spurious solutions which absolve them from acting or taking sudden risks. More precisely, England was handicapped by her fear of Bolshevism, and, in England, specifically three elements, closely linked to each other: the venerable conservatives in Parliament, the aristocracy, the City. When only one last fillip was needed to overthrow Mussolini, all these people said to themselves with a spasm of fear: "But then? . . . What's going to happen? What will replace Fascism in Italy? Bolshevism almost certainly . . . or anarchy tending towards Bolshevism, which Russia will immediately exploit. . . . And as Mussolini's fall will almost immediately provoke Hitler's, the same appalling regime will rise in Germany. . . . And as we already hear things aren't going so well in Spain, where the government is letting the Reds get out of hand, it may be the end of everything . . . and we'd be the ones, we good conservatives, good aristocrats, good English capitalists, to let all hell loose? . . ." And they shrank back in terror. They didn't picture in the least the siege of England by the Nazis, or the bombing of London. . . . Venerable conservatives lack imagination.

Their distress was voiced in a question put to the royal house of Italy through confidential channels which it is not impossible to identify: "Suppose Mussolini falls, will the House of Savoy take the responsibility of maintaining order in Italy for a fortnight?" That first fortnight over, the worst dangers, it was hoped, would have been averted. The new government, already provisionally made up, would have had time to organize itself, decide on its first acts of authority, and take charge of the situation. But England didn't want the responsibility of the first fortnight. The royal house answered, we're told, that it couldn't give such a guarantee. Its fears apparently centred less on disturbances of Bolshevist inspiration than on acts of violence which the "desperate" among the Fascists might perpetrate *"in extremis"*, for though they numbered only ten to fifteen thousand, nevertheless they had ample means to do great harm. The very urgent task which was expected of the royal house would have been facilitated if the Prince of Piedmont, heir to the crown, had been more popular. But he wasn't liked, especially in Rome, where he was accused of leading the life of a *"fêtard"*—a rake (he's mended his ways since then, they say).

Of course, it's difficult to dispel all uncertainty as to the dates of these events and the exact purport of the words used. Only those directly concerned could do so, if they had a mind to, and if their memories were accurate. But it's wiser not to count on either of these happenings.

This is where the problem of Leopold III's intervention comes up, an intervention which is very likely
to be kept dark. It is certain that he took a trip to
England at that time; it's probable he took more than
one. (The young sovereign travelled around more
often than the good Belgian public ever realized, and
he had a liking for being incognito.) We're told he
undertook to transmit to London, especially to the
Prince of Wales, who a few weeks later was to become
Edward VIII, a kind of dynastic S O S: "Look out!
You're going to overthrow, not Mussolini only, but
the House of Savoy! It may be the beginning of a new
collapse of European dynasties. Don't go and sacrifice blindly all that's left of order and tradition to the
Geneva ideology." Leopold's family connection with
the royal house of Italy gave his message more weight.
Moreover, he was not at all averse to bearing it, for
though he was a friend of peace, he was also a friend
of authority, and he belonged to the set of young sovereigns, or future sovereigns, who would have been
pleased to see, in each one of their countries, the establishment of a modified Fascism, a Fascism without
Mussolini, which would have been in their control.
I hope that some day someone will be in a position to
write the story of that coterie which more than once
conspired, and whose role is not to be overlooked,
even though some of its members fell on bad days. In
it we should have to place, besides Leopold III, the

ephemeral Edward VIII, King Carol, not ephemeral but intermittent, perhaps Boris of Bulgaria as "associate member", and Prince Paul, Regent of Yugoslavia; it's probable that between two "sprees" the Prince of Piedmont sent the little set signals of friendship, if not of distress.

Summing things up: the answer to the question: "Who saved Fascism?" must be: First of all, Pierre Laval (and it's not without reason that in his little book, *A New Holy Alliance*, Emil Ludwig stated in 1938 that if a new European war broke out, one of the men most responsible would be Pierre Laval); in the second place, broadly speaking, the English conservatives, blinded by their terror of Bolshevism; and last, as accessory, the little dynastic plot of which Leopold was the spokesman.

What motivated the English conservatives, or Leopold III, in this case is too evident to call for explanation. Pierre Laval's case is psychologically more complex.

Did he deliberately mean to destroy peace and the interests of France? Did he realize that by saving Mussolini and European Fascism he was sending Europe headlong into war after a more or less brief respite; that he was calling the forces of death and destruction upon his country, and perhaps an irreparable defeat? Certainly not. It's quite possible, even, that he thought he'd managed for the best, always taking his personal position into account, and in full measure. At the beginning of 1935 he had gone to Rome fondly hoping to conquer Mussolini. He had made Mussolini promises the implication and gravity of which he did not realize until later on. The two men had liked each other. A kind of friendship had grown up between them. Then when the Ethiopian affair went badly, Laval felt tied to Mussolini by an obligation of a personal kind: "I can't do that to him now! . . . It would be a caddish trick!" And he was one of those men for whom a bond of that kind counted more than abstract morality, or ideas; one of those men, too, who don't like to see the tragic side of a situation, and who wish to convince themselves that in the end things will come out all right after a great deal of vociferation, as in deals between peasants. Besides, he could flatter himself that he was following, if not a system, at least a policy: making a friend of Italy once more so as to keep Germany within bounds.

Even now I'm not sure whether he has weighed his responsibility. He may even say to himself: "If only they'd listened to me more . . . if only they hadn't irritated Mussolini uselessly. . . ." Of course, that's only the sophism of a man who tries to clear himself before his own conscience—and before history—and who besides is a lawyer by profession; for since then he has been obliged to see, like everyone else, that

251

Mussolini hadn't the least gratitude to France for what she did at the time not to down him, or even to save him; that on the contrary he came out of the affair with renewed spite—like a man whose head has been held under water, and who'll never forgive the terrible scare you gave him, nor the humiliating grace you granted by loosening your grip.

Besides, what goes on in M. Laval's conscience matters little. By deliberately saving Fascism, he, alas, more than anyone else in France is the author of the 1939 catastrophe and of the disaster suffered by his country.

From that very moment war was practically inevitable. Great statesmanship was no longer possible. It was the League's death-blow. We had to borrow short at high interest, and strain our wits to postpone payment. All the opportunities for opposing Fascism which apparently offered themselves were poor opportunities. Oh, certainly, we who fought for peace tried not to admit all this so as to keep up our courage. But sometimes we admitted it in spite of ourselves: as when in October 1938, after Munich, I exclaimed, at a congress of war veterans: "They tell us Munich is a capitulation. But it was at the end of 1935 that the giant capitulation, the irreparable one, took place! All the others stemmed from it!"

Yes, all the others, even including that of King Leopold III in the open field, even including that of France in June 1940.

The democracies should draw more than one lesson from this—if lessons can still be of use.

First, they must admit that they betrayed themselves by reprieving an implacable enemy who was out to assassinate them, reprieving him out of cowardice, out of questionable indulgence, or in submission to false fears.

Then, they must also admit that certain opportunities can never be recaptured. Opportunities which, seized, save uncounted efforts—not to speak of catastrophes—but once they are rejected, uncounted efforts lavished from day to day will not succeed in regaining what was lost in one move.

They must at last admit—all the democracies, and, above all, those which have not yet suffered the crucial tests—that those great opportunities, the royal graces granted us by destiny, are always recognizable, quite recognizable. To discover them, we do not need supernatural penetration; we need only to open our eyes.

A NOTE ON THE TYPE

The text of this book is set in Caledonia, a new Lino-type face designed by W. A. Dwiggins. Caledonia belongs to the family of printing types called "mod-ern face" by printers—a term used to mark the change in style of type-letters that occurred about 1800. Caledonia is in the general neighborhood of Scotch Modern in design, but is more freely drawn than that letter.

The book was composed, printed, and bound by H. Wolff, New York. The paper was made by S. D. Warren Company, Boston.